CW01572243

Best Wishes from

Cassie & Catherine

Caroline Milton was educated at three convents, both Roman and Anglo Catholic, subsequently attending university where she read English. She worked for a short time in London before marrying a soldier and spending the next two decades travelling and living abroad in the Far East, Africa and Europe while bringing up a family of three. On returning to England, she worked as P.A. to a Member of Parliament during which time she became interested in esoteric subjects.

As an army daughter *Cassie Martin* had a childhood of travel, sun and warm seas. A year was spent at university studying history after which she worked in London where she met her husband. For six years she worked as a secretary for the World Health Organisation in Geneva, where she developed an interest in astrology and spiritual books at the same time as Caroline. She returned to the UK to bring up her two daughters.

RING QUEST

The Continuing Story of the Ring

Cassie Martin and Caroline Milton

© 2007 Cassie Martin and Caroline Milton

All rights reserved.
No part of this publication may be reproduced,
stored in a retrieval system, or transmitted in any
form or by any means, without the prior permission in
writing of the publisher, nor be otherwise circulated in any
form of binding or cover other than that in which it is
published and without a similar condition including this
condition being imposed on the subsequent purchaser.

ISBN 978-1-84799-763-0

Printed by Lulu.com

This book is dedicated to Robert Light
without whom it would not have been written.

Acknowledgements

We would like to thank our families and all those friends who, over the years while this book was being both written and re-enacted, gave us their support and encouragement. We would also like to thank Darren Bowden for the design of the book cover, and Maria Burns for her illustrations of the Signs of the Zodiac.

Contents

Illustrations of Astrological Signs in London

The Road goes on forever following the Ring

Introduction

The light was dim in the early hours of the morning as a lorry drove slowly up the hill one spring day in the 1970's in Badby, Northamptonshire. In the middle of the road stood a white horse. As the lorry driver drew closer he could make out a woman in an old-fashioned white dress mounted on the horse staring at the lorry. It was only when the vehicle was 15 feet away and the driver had just opened the door to get out and ask the lady to move that the horse suddenly jumped over the hedge. There was no sound of horse's hooves, just the rustling of bushes. So real was the apparition that, instinctively, the driver got out of the lorry and climbed on some bricks to get a better view over the hedge of the horse and rider. But there was nothing to be seen.

He later discovered the woman to be the ghost of Mrs Fitzgerald who had been murdered by her husband as she returned home on her white horse from an illicit meeting with her lover. Her husband was waiting for her in the servants' quarters with a shotgun and shot her dead. Such traumatic circumstances can very often result in the person being trapped at the low astral level, in that time, repeating the tragic events that led to their deaths. It is moving to speculate that when her horse died it chose to remain with its mistress out of love and because of the mistress's need for companionship. Her faithful horse must have been of great comfort to Mrs Fitzgerald in her desolate state.

As so often in such examples of ghostly re-enactment, the person who saw the ghostly pair thought they were real. The story implies that at another, finer level people are still caught up in events that took place a long time ago and should by rights have ended. Yet these souls appear trapped and hopelessly bound to repeat them in order to try and change the outcome. We are affected by the emotional imprint of past events left in the ether around us, even to the extent of it adversely affecting our health.

As many know, there is an interaction between our physical world and those other dimensions on certain anniversaries. Laurence Gardner (author of the well-known *Bloodline of the Holy Grail*) says in his book *Lost Secrets of the Sacred Ark* that modern scientists have '....confirmed the existence of parallel dimensions..' and that these scientists have '..expressed their particular concern that the public are kept in the dark about such matters.'

Our story pushes out the boundaries of our understanding a little further. In 1997 a man called Robert Light entered our lives. He has extraordinary powers, of which there are many examples throughout this book. He sets us off on a quest, in which he himself plays a vital part, to change a story - a true one - that has repeatedly been re-enacted at that finer level at the end of every Age, where we once again find ourselves. Those events are then bound to be played out at the dense physical level because of the old saying: 'As above, so below'. The story we were to work with was J.R.R. Tolkien's trilogy, *The Lord of the Rings*. It can be no coincidence that the book has now been turned into an epic film, catching the attention of many millions of people all over the world.

A group of us was told by Robert that by consciously earthing the Story at the dense physical level, we have the ability to clear the ether of the ghost of our past. Those energies, of good and evil, of great deeds and battles fought swirling around us at other dimensions, which would then be cleared to the benefit of humankind. That change can only be made from the physical level where we are not trapped within those events. We were also told that through our ability, consciously, to interact with those events, we can change the Story and so bring about a satisfactory resolution.

Why should we need to change the Story, we wondered and, for that matter, why has the Story continued to be recycled? The answer came from Robert that humanity had not learnt its lessons and has continued to repeat the same mistakes. Had the Evil Ring of Power made by the Dark Lord truly been destroyed when it fell into the fiery abyss of the volcano? And if not, what would have been the consequences? Apparently, we are at a unique time in our history where we have the opportunity to get the Story right at those higher levels. Everything is coming together – the past, present and the future. We are at the End Times.

There is a belief in some circles that our planet is undergoing great changes and that its vibrations are rising, as well as the vibrations of all life on the planet, including ourselves, if we choose. If this is the case, would we not get a nasty shock if the veil that presently separates us from unseen worlds were suddenly removed? There might be horrors that we would rather not see. In this light, the work that our group and others are doing to clear those levels first, suddenly makes a lot of sense. Also, in order for the planet to raise its vibrations, it is necessary to clear the enveloping black miasma which some books have described and which prevents the light penetrating.

The authors of *The Green Stone* (Graham Phillips, Martin Keatman) and others were also involved in a story, which connected with evil at the astral level in a very real way, just as ours does. They enter a story whose origins go back in time to Egypt and the Pharaoh Akhenaton. It centres round a stone of great power and a direct confrontation with the Evil One.

With the benefit of hindsight, we can see that both groups had a period of preparation so that our minds were open to ideas which many would have dismissed out of hand. Some of the participants in the story of *The Green Stone* came to their experiences via research into UFO's, which took them straight into their amazing adventures.

We began in a small way, some seven years before the start of this story. After picking up the idea from a book in January 1991, we decided to test our possible powers of dowsing. This soon led on to clearing areas of negativity, particularly churches on energy lines in and around Northampton. Cassie lived in Northampton with her husband and two small daughters. Caroline, Cassie's mother, was in London at the time but used to travel regularly to Northampton to help out with the two girls. Later, a book on ghost stories of Northamptonshire made us focus for a while on releasing trapped souls.

We found the free flow of energy at churches along the energy lines was often blocked. There were varying causes for this but one which we discovered was due to the practices of the pagan cult of worship of the Goddess. Cassie had been researching the pagan cults and she discovered that their focus was the supposed life-giving powers of the King. This resulted in his sacrifice twice yearly, at mid-summer and mid-winter, so that the community could benefit from those life-giving powers in a most gruesome manner. With tragic consequences for women, he was sacrificed in the name of the all-powerful Queen who was considered the Goddess's representative. We discovered that successive sacrifices took place at the same place, and that these sites were also energy centres where several energy/ley lines cross and there is underground water. It was on such sites that many pre-reformation churches and cathedrals were built.

The negative energy at these power points would have begun to build up with successive sacrifices so that souls became trapped at such places. Cassie has written about how we made this discovery in another book. We were so moved by the cruel end of so many young men that we began travelling the country visiting cathedrals, churches, hill forts, abbeys and castles, which are on sites of former pagan worship, releasing these trapped souls.

We were blithely unaware that such work involved very real dangers, as we were drawing attention to ourselves from what you might call the 'evil forces'. It is from such centres of polluted energy that they draw much of their power. To see that energy being transmuted into positive energy was not to their liking. At this point, in the summer of 1998, through a friend of Caroline's who lives in the Wye valley, we began attending self-awareness workshops in Lydney, Gloucestershire, given by Robert Light who astonished us with his knowledge of our activities without our having mentioned them to him. He pointed out that we were working at a more powerful level now which took us beyond his protection and that we had gone into some very dangerous places. Caroline remarked that we must have gone where Angels fear to tread and Robert, smilingly, agreed. We needed to learn to protect ourselves.

Unfortunately, mention of active forces for evil in the world today can have the effect of making some people automatically consign any such book to the realms of science fiction. Yet it has to be acknowledged that we live in a world of polarity – of light and dark, masculine and feminine, East and West, good and evil. In fact, the one cannot exist without the other. In C.S. Lewis's book *The Screwtape Letters* the senior devil tells the junior devil that their supreme weapon is that nobody believes they exist.

The adventures and experiences in this book are real and we, as a group, have as our guide a most remarkable man. We were made aware that we would encounter opposition and we needed to be alert to this. We also knew that the worst thing was to have fear. For this reason we thought it best not to dwell on the danger. The downside to our approach sometimes meant, unfortunately, that we were negligent in protecting ourselves and in picking up the signs around us which link the two worlds. It was easy enough to be aware when we were very deliberately stepping into the Story but less so when immersed in our everyday lives.

Tolkien

In bookshops Tolkien's books are put on the "Fantasy" shelves. However, it cannot be denied that *The Lord of the Rings* has profoundly affected many people the world over and has sold in its millions. If Tolkien's writings were just fantasy would they have drawn such responses as the one from a college student: *"The Lord of the Rings* was and will probably be the most significant book of my life." Patrick Curry, a great admirer of Tolkien's work, wrote a book called *Defending Middle Earth* based on the idea that the Story is relevant to us today. He writes that on first reading *The Lord of the Rings* at the age of sixteen, "I was overcome from the beginning by the unmistakable sense of having encountered a world that was more real than the one I was then living in .....Accompanying this feeling was the equally odd one of inexplicable familiarity with that world."

Many new ideas have come 'out of the blue' and have not been the product of the logical, deductive process. Einstein said that his ideas on Relativity came suddenly to him out of nowhere. Composers will hear the music in their heads, perfectly formed, and all they have to do is write it down. This can be called 'inspired' or, dare one say it, given to us from a higher level from whatever benign source.

Later, Tolkien himself came to believe that the story he had written was true. He says that he 'was drawn irresistibly' to certain things and that 'discovery' felt much more the case than 'invention' and that 'the story unfolded itself as it were'. The American writer, Clive Kilby, who spent three months in the summer of 1966 working closely with Tolkien, writes in his book *Tolkien and The Silmarillion* (1976) of an extraordinary incident when a Member of Parliament visiting Tolkien in his home declared, "<u>You</u> did not write *The Lord of the Rings*," meaning that it had been given him from God. It was clear that he (Tolkien) favoured this remark.'

If such is the case, the question arises, 'for what purpose?' Could such an involved story, which many find so gripping and powerful, be anything other than the true history of Man? When people say Tolkien derived his tales from the Anglo Saxon, Gothic and Norse Mythology, could it in fact be the other way round? Legends, mythologies and fairy stories have come down to us from the tales Tolkien relates and are but windows on our remote past. With Tolkien, we get the original story.

The Cult of the Goddess and the Sacred King

A brief outline of this Cult is necessary for a fuller understanding of our Quest. In the pagan religious cults, it was the Queen who ruled in the name of the all-powerful Goddess on whose fertility the community's very survival depended. Her consort, the Divine Sun King, was the embodiment of the sun and for her continuing abundant fertility both she and the earth had to be fertilised by the glorious Sun King. It was believed that the power of the sun built up in the very body of the King as the sun ascended to its zenith at midsummer, when he too, like the sun was at full power. On that day he was sacrificed, in the name of the Queen/Goddess, on a high place – a hill or mountain - and his body and blood were used to bless and fertilise the land and the people. There were two Kings, one for the Waxing Year and one for the Waning Year. Upon the sacrifice of the first, his twin, or 'King-in-waiting' took his place. As the sun began its descent in the skies, the King's strength likewise was perceived to decline. Finally, at midwinter the sun was seen to 'die' and the King of the Waning Year was also put to death. His sacrifice took place in a sacred grove of trees, marshland or underground. The sun had returned to the very womb of the Goddess from whom he was reborn as the 'New' Sun King as, once again, the sun began to ascend the sky and the grisly cycle was repeated.[1]

Grotesquely, for all its seeming emphasis on the life-giving qualities of the semi-divine Sun King, the cult was, in reality, a Death Cult, as the focus of the religious year was the sacrifice of the Kings at mid-summer and mid-winter.

Cassie's source also makes it absolutely clear that this practice was worldwide. Perhaps the reason for this is that the original, uncorrupted ideas on which the Cult was based, came out of Atlantis and were taken to the different corners of the earth by refugees fleeing the destruction of that island.

It was to be many years before we realised that the Cult was an integral part of our Quest.

---

[1] See historical research in Appendices

Chapter 1

The One Ring Remade

"The One Ring has remade itself and is exerting an evil influence in the world today"? we repeated incredulously to Robert who had just made this outrageous statement. He was referring to none other than the Ring of Power forged by the Dark Lord, Sauron, in J.R.R. Tolkien's book *The Lord of the Rings*. Naturally, we were aghast at such a suggestion, but not disbelieving because we had come to know Robert over the past year and knew that he was quite capable of making such a statement in all seriousness. We were also in no doubt as to the truth of this extraordinary idea.

We had been attending Robert's self-awareness workshops held in the library at Lydney on the edge of the Forest of Dean,, making the long journey from Northampton. For some time before that a group of us used to get together at the weekends at the house of a friend of Caroline's nearby. We had similar 'New Age' interests, as they were then called, in such subjects as hands on healing and self-awareness. It was Enid, a member of this group, who first went to one of Robert's self-awareness workshops and strongly recommended them to us. We found his teaching to be different from anything we had experienced before - it was simple, yet at the same time, mind-stretching, a sort of 'back to basics' spirituality that had existed before man forgot his interconnectedness with All that Is.

To begin with, his teaching focussed on simple things like being grounded and balanced for which he used the image of a daisy. The daisy is a beautifully simple, yet effective, idea. The white petals and yellow centre represent the principles of feminine and masculine so that balance is quickly acquired, and the roots of the flower give the necessary grounding. He would ask us to visualise our daisy. Cassie can remember how she visualised hers the first time as a tall, thin-stemmed version and how it drooped easily. He used to go round advising everyone in the circle in turn. He looked at her, when it came to her turn, and told her somewhat tersely that a daisy was a hardy flower and close to the ground. Thereafter she saw it as short-stemmed, sturdily taking the buffeting of any winds. Caroline, much to her surprise, was told that she was floating a foot above the ground and, obviously, needed to 'ground' herself.

For emotional wellbeing we were to visualise a rose. Robert's comment, when it came to Cassie's turn, was uncannily accurate. It was clear to her that he was able to see the image she was holding in her mind. She realised with a shock just how accurate her own subconscious mind was in throwing up a rose in that particular state of bloom. For physical strength we were asked to visualise a tree. We could then draw up energy from the roots and energy down from the sun where they would intermingle in the middle, around the area of the solar plexus.

From such experiences, we realised that Robert had extra-ordinary gifts.

It was July 1998 and five of us were sitting in Enid's sitting room in her house in Lydney, close to The Forest of Dean, when Robert dropped his bombshell about the Ring of the Dark Lord exercising an evil power in our world today. He had arranged this particular meeting saying it was important but only a few people were free to attend. There were four of us: Enid, Clarissa, Caroline and Cassie. Several topics were discussed but all we have recorded and can remember now is what was to set us all off on an extraordinary adventure.

Robert quite suddenly changed the conversation and asked us about the history of the planet and of Man and what life had been like on this planet in the remote past. We did our best to answer these unexpectedly profound questions and finally suggested that life had been at the etheric level. The etheric is still part of the physical world but vibrating at a higher level, which we cannot yet see until such time as we are able to raise our own vibrations. He went on to say that the story of *The Lord of the Rings* was a true one that had taken place about sixty thousand years ago and that Tolkien's book had been 'inspired'.

The Ring of Power had not been completely destroyed when it fell into the fiery abyss with Gollum; it had only been destroyed in one of the elements, that of fire. Sauron had made the One Ring in all the elements – earth, water, air, fire and ether so that it might have power in the land of the living. When it was thrown into fire, therefore, it was not fully 'unmade'. This meant it could reconstitute itself at the end of an Age when its master, Sauron, re-emerging from the

Shadows, began to grow in power once again and bend his mind and will to finding the lost Master Ring. This 'awoke' the latent malice of the Ring, which in turn began actively seeking its Master.

We learnt that the Story has been repeated many times at the end of every Age because "Man had not learnt his lessons." We were only vaguely aware of what those lessons might be. It seemed to us that Tolkien himself tells us humankind's weaknesses. One is that we are easily enamoured of the Dark Arts and many people worshipped the Dark Lord then - as they still do today. Another, was that men's wills quickly submitted to the power of the other Rings forged by Sauron. Nine of these were given to proud and powerful kings who became the 'living dead', called the Nazgul or Ringwraiths (also the Black Riders) in the story of *The Lord of the Rings*.

Even Frodo and Samwise's Quest to throw the One Ring into the fires of Mount Doom is already a second attempt to destroy the Ring. The earlier attempt had failed due to Man's weakness of will.[1] The opportunity is missed and therefore Sauron is incompletely defeated, only to rise and, once again, attempt world domination at the end of yet another Age. The customary way evil lures people into its service is through greed and the lust for power. There is evidence aplenty of this in our present world. These must be some of the lessons that we have not yet learnt.

Later on at home, when we were still trying to work things out, we telephoned Robert and he told us that we had to think harder about Man's journey to the present day. This made us realise that we have to go back the way we came, which means we must return to the etheric level of existence. The fall in the earth's energy level, or slowing down of the vibrations, which occurs at the end of the story in *The Lord of the Rings,* is a subtle current throughout the book.[2] Sauron's defeat at the end of the Story means that he will sink so low that he will not be able to take form again in the world of the living. But, if Robert is to be believed, Sauron is still trying to exercise a malevolent power over us from the lower astral levels, or the Regions of Hell, as the Christians would call them, as the replay button is pressed once again.[3]

This time around, we are being made aware of the wider reality we live in, although some may deny such truth. If we can 'detect the signs of the Story of *The Lord of the Rings* interacting with our world we can, uniquely, ground it through being consciously aware of what is taking place at that other level. This gives us the opportunity to change it, get it right and clear it from that level once and for all.

Chapter 2

The Eye of Surveillance

What evidence is there to suggest that the Ring of Power is influencing our world? And what evidence is there that the story in *The Lord of the Rings* is being played out again at another level, as Robert has suggested?

Walking down the street in any town in the country in May 1999, it wouldn't take long to come across a poster of the latest Star Wars Film. Cassie found herself staring with growing disbelief at the image of Liam Neeson as Obi One Kenobi, holding up a light sabre as if it were a shining sword. She took in his long brown hair, the plain brown clothes, the eagle-like nose and the grim expression. Here was a man who fitted the description of Aragorn, the King-in-waiting in the story of *The Lord of the Rings*, in a most uncanny way. He also held a great sword: Aragorn was the wielder of the great sword Anduril, Flame of the West. There were other posters advertising the film *Godzilla*, which showed just one large, menacing eye. If Liam Neeson was Aragorn, this was the Eye of Sauron. Later, when re-reading the description of Sauron's Eye in Tolkien's book, the comparison was confirmed: it was an exact description of the Eye of Godzilla - yellow with a black slit for a pupil.

Most amazing of all was the timing. These films were being shown at the end of a millennium to coincide with the original Story being re-activated once again at other levels which means, according to the law of 'as above so below', that the Story will impress itself upon our world. Here was proof that this was already happening.

The ever-watchful Eye of Sauron is present in many ways. It occurred to us that television, cinema, computer screens and CCTV cameras all share characteristics of The Eye. They even have the optic nerve, which is the electrical wiring. The moving, watchful eye of surveillance cameras can be directly compared with the ranging Eye of Sauron as he monitored developments in the world far and wide.

Television creates an artificial world and in recent years we have increasingly been fed an artificial diet of sex and violence. Video games have taken the violence to new extremes. Even the expression for the internet as 'the worldwide web' aroused our suspicions, as it brought to mind the giant evil spider, Shelob, in the Story. She very nearly killed and devoured Frodo, the Ringbearer, on his seemingly hopeless quest. The Web, of course, is a very useful resource but it can also be put to evil use through the misuse of 'chat rooms' and exchange of pornographic material, Again, it can create an artificial world cut off from social interaction and relationships, as well as from he natural world.

Sauron's powers of surveillance can partly be attributed to possessing one of the Seven Stones of Seeing which resemble the gypsy's crystal ball.[4]   Only Saruman and Denethor, Steward of Gondor, in addition to Sauron, possessed this powerful but dangerous tool. The other Stones had been lost during the many wars. Both men, in their different ways succumbed to the will of Sauron. When Denethor looked into the crystal ball, he only saw what Sauron wished him to see, which was the military strength of the Dark Lord, beyond count. This slowly poisoned the mind of Denethor and he succumbed to the evil of despair and hopelessness. To a large extent we have no control over what is fed to us on television and many of us are alert to this and protest about the foul language and violence. More recently, people have been concerned with the 'dumbing down' in the programmes on offer. In other words, we are being given a distorted view of world affairs, just as Sauron gave a distorted view to Denethor.

Robert told us of how, when asked to see if he could help a family which was having problems, he walked into the house and removed the television. A week later, peace had descended on the household. Instead of watching television constantly, which made them subtly bored and irritable, and was the cause of outbursts of violent temper, they had been forced to find something creative to do with their free time. Most of us do manage to be selective and have a balance. But are many of us, like Denethor, endlessly shown selective scenes of violence in the trouble spots of the world, in danger of succumbing to a feeling of helplessness?

We can remember the moment when the significance of 'ring' roads struck us. There has been a proliferation of these in recent years in order to remove traffic from town centres. When Cassie next looked at a map she noticed that these 'ring' roads, such as the M25, actually resemble gigantic spiders: the roads leading into them looking remarkably like the legs of a spider. The extra large spider sitting over London could be likened to Shelob in the Story, and the smaller ones, crouching over the lesser cities, are her offspring. It is therefore not surprising that we get 'road rage' if we think that these black, tarmac 'rings' and roads are being used to channel evil energy from another level. The One Ring was created to control all the other Rings and all, therefore, became evil.[5] The powerful men who wore them were subverted and eventually controlled by Sauron's will, all except for the dwarves. Only the three Elven Rings were free. They had been forged in secret without Sauron's knowledge.

In a telephone conversation with Robert in the summer of 1999 Robert said something rather staggering, which shows in the most graphic way that history repeats itself. He said that the White House in the United States of America is Minas Tirith with its white tower, and Mordor is Afghanistan. However, the major players are not yet in place. Just as in Tolkien's story there is the division of East and West, so is it the case in our times. He identified The Fens with the Dead Marshes, which Frodo and Samwise crossed with Gollum as their guide. The Forest of Dean is the Shire – not so far from our meeting place - and the New Forest is the Forest of Fangorn.

In *The Lord of the Rings* we learn of the superior Numenorean race of men. They were exceptionally tall, black haired and grey-eyed. Their superiority also lay in their exceptional abilities – they had bright eyes with particularly acute eyesight, great physical strength and endurance, exceptional hearing and the gift of foresight. Aragorn, the future king, was of this race of men and one of his names was Thorongil, which means 'eagle-eyed'. Has anyone ever given a thought as to the origins of Superman? He clearly belongs to a superior race of men. But why is he always dark haired and blue eyed and never blonde and blue-eyed? We realised that his origins are most probably Numenorean. For us this was yet further evidence of the truth of Tolkien's story.

As if to press home the difference between the races found in the story of *The Lord of the Rings*, among the television presenters at Ascot this year (2006) was the extraordinary sight of ex-jockey, Willy Carson, who is extremely short, standing beside the statuesque model Jodie Kidd. There is a spectacular difference in height: they really do look like two different races. Willy Carson resembles a hobbit or 'halfling', not only in height, but he has the round face and is unquenchably cheerful and talkative – just like Tolkien's description of hobbits.

Most profound of all is the description of the Ring itself, as a plain, gold band without a gem. It suddenly dawned on us that this exactly describes the wedding ring. Can this be mere coincidence? Wouldn't it be fair to say that the married state, for women certainly, has often been a source of cruelty and tyranny? This has been truer the higher up the social scale you go. It was not so long ago, even in the West, that a husband had absolute jurisdiction over his wife, and his wife's property became his on their marriage. The absolute power a husband wields over his wife still persists in many countries today. Nor was it uncommon for men to change character for the worse on becoming married. We have all heard stories of how husbands begin to abuse their wives verbally and physically abuse, having given no indication of being capable of such behaviour during the period of courtship. There are examples in literature such as in Charles Dickens' *David Copperfield*. Does it suggest that the evil power of the One Ring is operating through those plain gold wedding bands (the word 'band' implies restriction)?

We then realised with amazement that the engagement ring, with its gem, so often either of sapphire, ruby or diamond, exactly resembles the Three Elven Rings in the story of *The Lord of the Rings*. Elrond wore the Ring with the blue stone - sapphire, Gandalf, the red stone – ruby, and Galadriel the clear stone of adamant - diamond. The period of courtship seems to reflect the good energy of those rings, being a period of happiness, excitement and hope for the future.

This difference between the two states – that of being engaged and that of being married – is reflected in astrology. The love planet, Venus, is said by astrologers to cast her beneficent influence during the period of betrothal. On becoming married, the relationship then comes under the harsh rule of Saturn, with its qualities of duty, cold reserve and restriction, not to mention criticism.

Chapter 3

St Dunstan's Church and Two Templar Forges in the City of London

It is not Robert's way to tell us very much: he expects us to work things out for ourselves. If we flounder for too long he gives us further clues. However, in retrospect, we were often too passive, which is one of the dangers in the teacher/pupil relationship. So, first of all we understood we were to 'destroy' the Ring, then we found out later from Robert that our actions would in fact be cleansing it, rather than destroying it.

How were we to accomplish such a cleansing? First we needed to locate the One Ring. This much we did understand: that Sauron's Ring is operating from the etheric level. The answer was to find a place of power. Because of the interaction between the two dimensions – physical and etheric – we would be able to call the One Ring to us. Our understanding was that, because we were the ones at the dense physical, we had the greater power. We are not trapped in the Story, so we are in a position to change it. Incidentally, Robert said something rather interesting. There are other stories, which other people are involved in, but this is the Story we are working with.

The idea of places where there is a concentration of energy is not a new one. In the course of dowsing two major energy lines in Britain, the authors of *The Sun and The Serpent,*

Hamish Miller and Paul Broadhurst, write about special energy sites where two or more energy lines cross. As mentioned in the introduction, for a number of years we had ourselves been involved with clearing pre-reformation churches and cathedrals, as well as hill forts which, as many people know, are built on power points and energy lines.

All we had to go by was that the Ring needed to be thrown into a fire, that the site would be somewhere near Holborn in London, and that twelve people would be involved. Caroline had just moved back to London and so was able to launch herself into the research.

Unfortunately, Robert was obliged to furnish us with more information. We had got nowhere as we were being too literal. Caroline had drawn up a list of all working glaziers in London from the local library but it turned out that the fire was an ancient forge no longer at the gross, physical level, but still existing at the etheric, and that it would be at the centre of a six-pointed star, the Star of David. The connection between the six pointed Star of David and kingship set us thinking that this was also the Star of Elendil, symbol of the Royal Line of Numenor, and that the Line of David was none other than its continuation. In Tolkien's Story it was foretold that the Line of Luthien (which became the Royal Line of Numenor) would never die out. Aragorn was the proof of this, stepping out of obscurity to claim the kingship in direct line from the last King, despite a lapse in kingship of over a thousand years when the stewards ruled in the king's stead

Robert also told us that it would be located in one of the signs of the Zodiac, which was to be found in the centre of

London, in the same way as the twelve signs of the Zodiac are arranged around Glastonbury Tor in Somerset, and that we should look for the outline in the roads and landmarks of the old City of London. We decided that of the three Fire signs in the Zodiac it was most likely to be Leo whose planetary ruler is the Sun and connected with kingship. As for the twelve people, we discovered that they did not need to be there in person as long as they were with us in spirit. To do this we just needed to name them, which we did, choosing from friends and relations.

Caroline visited the Guildhall Library in the City, the British Library and the British Museum, taking copies of old maps and notes from various books on the history of London. Cassie had a book on the ancient mounds of London and, with its help, we were able to draw the Star of David locating its six points at places of power, three of which are ancient prehistoric mounds. Two of the Sacred Mounds are on the banks of the River Thames and are entirely artificial. One of them is the famous Tower of London with its moat, originally known as The Bryn Gwyn, or White or Holy Hill. There is a plan afoot to refill the moat in honour of the London Olympics. Two miles away on Thorney Island was the Tothill in Westminster not a trace of which now remains. However, the memory of the ancient "Place of Assembly" survives in the names of Tothill Street and Tothill fields ('Tot' means a sacred mound).[6] The third is a natural hill called the Penton ('pen' means head and 'ton' also means a sacred mound) although nothing remains of it today.

The centre, as Robert suggested, was on or near St. Dunstan's church in Fleet Street and Caroline's research revealed that two forges had formerly stood on either side of this church. They had originally belonged to the Knights Templar who possessed a field known as Ficket's Croft on the north side of Fleet Street by Temple Bar. The field was used for training, jousting and exercising of the horses and the forges were, specifically, armourers' forges. Smithies and blacksmiths have always been magical and there is a connection to be made here with Freemasonry, the Philosopher's Stone and the higher spiritual and mental vibrations anciently attributed to kings. Aragorn is a good example. His lifespan was three times that of mortal man and he possessed healing powers and insight into the future.

As Caroline researched and measured, she wandered through the courts and gardens of the Temple and surrounding areas and had a frugal lunch of rice cakes and grapes in Fountain's Court. She felt out of Time, and the rice cakes became the Waybread or Lembas of the Elves. She discovered that popular house signs were preserved in the names of the warren of courts leading off Fleet Street pointing to the masculine and feminine principles representing both Sacred Kingship and the Goddess: names such as The Three Kings, Apollo Court, Crown Court, Hind Court and Hare Place, the latter two being animals sacred to the Goddess. Since the dawn of time this had been a centre of masculine power, later usurped by worship of the Goddess although it is commonly thought that the female principle was the first gender to be deified by Man. Worship of the Goddess evolved because Man, having sunk down the levels and become childlike, in his ignorance of who he was and where he came from, felt the need of a protective and all-powerful mother figure.

At this point Cassie came up to London for a week's visit and we started doing things together. Poring over several maps, ancient and modern, we discovered a reasonable outline of a lion running along streets with names such as Kingsway, Worship Street, Apollo Street and Sun Street, indicating the symbolic connection between the lion, kingship and the sun and the 'worship' of the glorious Sun King as a semi-divine being. It is interesting to note that the roads Sun Street, Worship Street, Apollo Street and Old Street are all within the head of the lion. The head of the Sun King was deemed particularly sacred as it represented the sun itself. Old Street alludes to the Sun King becoming 'old' as the sun sank ever lower in the skies and 'died' at midwinter. How the sign of the Royal Lion came to be corrupted by the energy of the Cult of Sacrifice of the King and why some Kings became cruel tyrants, is another story.

The Lion faces due East from where the 'new' sun will rise (the name of the road forming the profile of the lion's head is Great Eastern Street). Most extraordinary of all was that the generative organs of the outline of the Lion were exactly at the site of the two forges either side of St. Dunstan's Church - which symbolism obviously needs no explanation. St. Dunstan, as well as being Abbot of Glastonbury, is also thepatron saint of goldsmiths and gold is symbolically connected with kingship.

LEO ~ the Lion

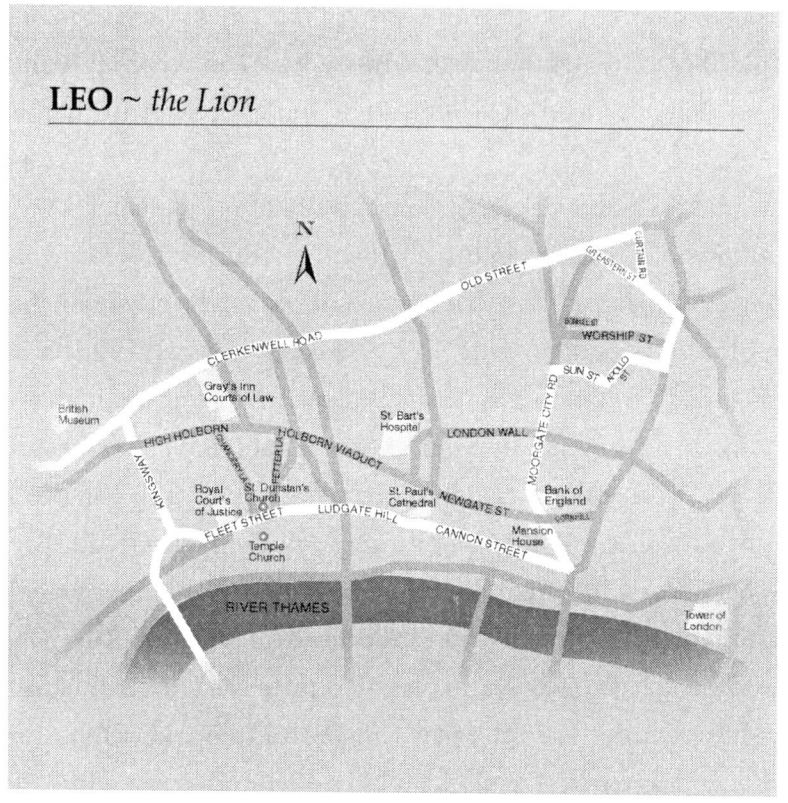

We can also expect to find the masculine emblems of power in an area permeated with the energy of the Lion, such as institutions connected with Law and Order. The Royal Courts of Justice, the highest Court in the land, is located there, as well as other Inns of Court nearby. The Nation's gold reserves are to be found within the golden Lion beneath The Bank of England.

However, in the past, these institutions have been used to oppress the people. The royal power was often unjust and cruel so we find in the vicinity such notorious prisons as Fleet Street and Newgate. We had noticed that the qualities, or energy, of the four Signs of the Zodiac we had discovered, spread beyond their outlines. Just outside the shape of the Lion, to the south and east, is the Tower of London - a Royal Palace, place of torture and imprisonment, and site of execution. But these were no ordinary prisoners: they were high ranking and often royal: Queen Anne Boleyn was beheaded there. It is interesting to note that beheading was reserved only for the nobility. It was the Sacred King too, who was beheaded so that his head might be worshipped at shrines for its prophesying powers, or sent rolling down the hill after his midsummer sacrifice.[2] The Mount, on which now stands the Keep, known as The White Tower, was clearly a former energy centre, which has been polluted by the Cult of Sacrifice of the King and the memory has lived on. It was also identified by Robert as the City of Minas Tirith in Tolkien's Story, Home to the Kings of the West, in the days before it became polluted.

---

[2] See historical notes in the Appendices

Chapter 4

'Smith Bernal Intl'

We were stirred into action when Robert suddenly said that things were getting to a critical point in the world and it was time to the find the Ring. We started getting some quite startling coincidences or synchronicities. We visited Watkins's Bookshop in Charing Cross and our eye fell on a book by Hamish Miller. It was called *Its Not Too Late* and on the cover was a huge and fiery ring. Towards the end of the story, when Frodo and Samwise are toiling across the parched wasteland surrounding the volcano, Frodo says his whole mind is filled with the image of a 'fiery Ring'. That evening there was a programme on television about volcanoes. In fact there were two programmes on television running at the same time called, respectively, *Savage Earth* and *Raging Planet* and it seemed that whenever we switched on the box there would be violent pictures of exploding mountains and fiery lava flows. Everywhere we went in London we again saw posters of a large and grizzly eye on the buses and in the shops advertising the film *Godzilla*: the unsleeping Eye of Sauron.

All that week the affairs of the world continued to deteriorate rapidly: the economic situation in Russia affecting the whole world economy, the Arab Fundamentalist attacks on US embassies in Kenya and Zambia, followed by the retaliatory attacks by the US on targets in the Sudan and

Afghanistan inflaming the whole of the Muslim world, including Pakistan with its nuclear arsenal, all culminating in the horrific bomb incident in Omagh.

It was the forge to the East of St Dunstan's, which turned out to be the right one and a most unpromising location it appeared to be when we went to check it out. We could see from behind the church from a raised level, a rather evil-looking, derelict house, blackened by soot, exactly like something out of Victorian London or a novel by Dickens. It was a strange sight in a built-up area in twentieth century London. To the East of this building was a tallish block of flats with what looked like a court between it and the derelict house. Our hopes lifted. We decided to try and reach it, if necessary, by getting into the block of flats. We walked into Fetter Lane and were relieved to find an archway leading into the court where there were a few parking places for cars from nearby firms. This was obviously the place and we rather desperately wondered where the exact spot of the furnace could be when Caroline noticed a plaque on the far wall. She walked across and there were the words 'SMITH BERNAL INTL', in other words, 'Smith, burn all internationally'. In this case, we knew that Smith was referring to a blacksmith, who would have worked in such a foundry hammering and welding the armour for the knights. The international part was referring to the worldwide effect it would have for reasons given below.

Underneath the plaque was a large, oblong slab of stone, like a hearthstone. We knew we had found the location of the forge's furnace at the etheric level where the fire was strong enough to cleanse the One Ring in the element of fire.

But what fairly took our breath away when we first saw the church was that the 'spire' was like a beautiful and delicate crown. It was as if someone in the Middle Ages knew the significance of this site when building the church. The only candidates who came to mind were the Templars. Even when they outgrew the site in High Holborn, they did not move far away, as evidenced by the Round Temple church just across the road about a hundred yards away. The Temple Church was consecrated in honour of the Blessed Virgin Mary on 10 February 1185 and was the chapel serving the London headquarters of the Knights Templar.

The power point we had decided upon where we would be able to summon the Ring, was the Royal Hospital Chapel, Chelsea. We had dowsed, as was our wont, to check that the chapel was on an energy centre, which it proved to be, and we cleared it of any negative energy. Robert had informed us over the telephone that we would have a guardian when we went to collect the Ring and that he would be wearing red.

May 2006. As we began to revise *Ring Quest* three years later, right on cue there appeared two programmes on television, within six days of each other, on two major natural disasters. The first one, *Krakatoa – The Last Days* (BBC1 on Sunday 7 May 2006), described the days leading up to the eruption of Krakatoa in Indonesia in 1845, which was the largest volcanic eruption in recent history. Sea levels were affected worldwide. The second, on BBC2's Timewatch, examined the story of the San Franciscan earthquake on April

18, 1906. It is described as America's biggest natural disaster: six thousand people were killed and the city all but completely destroyed.

Chapter 5

Link to Energy Centres Worldwide

Probably realising that we were not going to work it out for ourselves, Robert mentioned that the energy centre at St Dunstan's was linked to other places of power around the world. We surmised that they would also be masculine energy centres, as was St Dunstan's, and would therefore be sited on high places such as mountains. We also decided to match the number of sites with the 21 Rings of Power mentioned in Tolkien's books, which includes the Ruling Ring belonging to the Dark Lord. He had given seven rings to the dwarves, nine to men and three rings, made by the Elves, had been hidden from Sauron so that he knew nothing of them, although he suspected their existence.

Robert added that, when drawing the line from the centre in London, we had to take into account the curvature of the earth's surface! What a blow - our maths/geometry was not up to such calculations. We felt rather despondent but thought our best chance of finding out about these power points would be on the Internet. However, we drew a blank. Robert had given us a few places in England through which one or two of the energy lines would pass. We felt a great reluctance to go down that route, as the task felt too great. Much later it dawned on us that Robert knew all along that we wouldn't. Rather, he was providing the masculine balance, which is a more scientific approach whilst we provided the feminine, intuitive approach. In his talks he has stressed the need for this balance. We therefore started trying to find the places of power first and then working from the outside into the centre, thereby obviating the need to take the earth's curvature into consideration – something that was never going to happen!

We spent Sunday looking at a map of the world, which, curiously, mentioned the names of quite obscure mountains, which were to prove most helpful to us. We each began suggesting sites and were astonished at how many were well-known. We should not have been, as extra powerful energy sites such as these would have acted as a magnet. We finally had our twenty in a surprisingly short period of time, dowsing for confirmation: the Kremlin, the Vatican, the Potala Palace in Tibet (no wonder the Chinese want, or rather need that country), Mount Fuji, Ayers Rock, Mount Kilimanjaro, Glastonbury, the Parthenon, Golgotha in Jerusalem, Krak des Chevaliers in Syria, Angkor Wat, the Great Pyramid of Giza, the Royal Palace in Baghdad, Mount Whitney in California, Mount Teotihuacan in Mexico, Machu Picchu in Peru, the Buddhist Temple at Kandy, Ceylon, Jotunheiman in Norway, Montcalm in the Pyrenees and, finally, London at the centre. It is interesting to note that England has two sites, the other being Glastonbury, whereas the continents of North and South America have only one site each (if you count Mexico as Central America). Australia also has only a single site and the continent of Africa two. The vast majority, fourteen, are in Asia and Europe, seven in each.

Chapter 6

"Don't Forget the Ring"

We had one last synchronicity just the night before setting off to cleanse the One Ring for the first time. Caroline's husband turned on the television to watch the Bond film 'Licence to Kill' and the first words we heard were 'I hope you've remembered the ring'. As if we could forget it! Whoever, or whatever is creating these synchronicities – the universe responding to us most likely – has a sense of humour.

The sun was shining as we set off the following morning, 25th August 1999. We took a bus to the Royal Hospital and made our way to the Chapel and there we met our guardian. He was a Chelsea Pensioner and of course he was dressed in the traditional red frock coat. His name was William West and, after we had chatted to him for a while, he told us that he was the Pearly King of Chelsea and that we should bow to him! Here was our King. He pointed out a beautiful wooden panel above the altar on which was carved a sun with rays shooting from it. It is supposed to have been rescued from a church after the Great Fire of London. He then showed us a chair, which at the request of the Queen Mother was reconstructed from the debris of the panelling where a bomb had hit the Chapel. It was called 'The King's Chair'. Here then were the themes of the sun, fire and kingship, which were so fitting.

After talking to our Pearly King for a while longer we began to wonder how we would ever be able to call up the Ring in private, so Caroline rather desperately said: 'Now we would like to say a little prayer,' to which he replied, much to our consternation: 'You're joking'. Staunchly showing him we weren't and wondering if any visitors ever prayed in the Chapel, we walked towards the Choir stall, knelt down and shut our eyes hoping for a miracle. One duly happened. The telephone rang and he went to answer it. Feeling slightly silly, Caroline got out the white handkerchief (we thought white would be a counterbalance to the evil vibrations of the Ring) and placed it over the palm of her hand. We called three times, as planned, not too loudly, for the Ring to materialise on the handkerchief. Nothing happened and at that point our guardian reappeared. Stupidly, Caroline kept her hand out with the handkerchief still on it until she suddenly noticed that our King was eyeing it rather suspiciously. Hastily, she put it in her pocket and a second miracle happened: the telephone rang again. We then rather desperately repeated the performance and still nothing happened. With a sudden flash of inspiration Caroline realised that it would not materialise as a physical object, it would be present on the palm of the hand at the etheric level. Quickly she whipped off the handkerchief and this time felt a distinct tingling on her palm. She carefully tipped it onto the handkerchief, wrapped it up, and then placed it in the bag. With that we made a hasty exit before our guardian could reappear, feeling sorry that we were unable to say goodbye.

As we left, Caroline began to wonder if she would suddenly be overcome by the power of the Ring and refuse to relinquish it. Luckily, she felt reasonably calm. We made our way to Sloane Square and took the Circle Line to the Temple. From there we walked through the gardens, into Fleet Street, through the courts and alleyways of The Temple, until at last we were in the small parking area to the side of St Dunstan's church. Standing in front of the plaque and the hearthstone Caroline tossed the etheric ring into the air while we asked out loud for it to be cleansed in the fires of the furnace. We also sent the purified energy down the energy lines to the masculine centres of power worldwide so that they too would be cleansed. In her mind's eye Cassie saw a flame leap up, confirmation that we had been successful. Feeling both deeply satisfied and elated we decided to celebrate by going to the nearest café for coffee and croissants.

In the days following, events in the world took an upturn. Gerry Adams renounced violence – the negative side of the fiery energy - and then agreed to decommissioning of the IRA's arsenal, the Muslim world remained calm and the US and UK stock markets rallied. A week later the Real IRA renounced violence and there was an historic meeting between David Trimble, Northern Ireland's Prime Minister, and Gerry Adams, leader of Sin Fein. The week after that, Basque separatists in Catalan sought reconciliation with the Spanish Government and the ETA called for a ceasefire. On the 20th September Iraq dropped the Fatwa against Salman Rushdie.

Synchronicities continued. In the American sit-com *Friends* two of the young men, Chandler and Ross, are expecting a visit from an old college friend whose nickname is Gandalf, the 'party wizard', and one of the characters says, 'You remember Gandalf from the book *The Lord of the Rings*'? On a more sinister note there was a huge eye on the cover of one of the Sunday paper's magazines.

There was also a strange sequel. We had promised Cassie's two girls an outing the following day and two places had been suggested, Kensington Palace and the Zoo. However, at the last minute we changed our plans and decided on Madame Tussaud's and the Planetarium. It was warm and sunny day but later it became overcast. We all had an enjoyable time, although the room full of severed heads of those who had been decommissioned was weird, for it reminded us of our research into the pagan Cult of the Goddess. On leaving we walked along Euston Road intending to get a bus down Baker Street. As we passed Baker Street Underground station one of the girls said, "Shall we go on the Underground"? However, we decided that a journey by bus would be more fun. That evening we heard on the news that a man carrying a bomb had been apprehended at Warren Street Underground station which just happens to be the next station along from Baker Street. We felt glad that we hadn't after all taken the Underground and thought nothing more of it.

At our next meeting and workshop with Robert two months later, Caroline happened to mention this incident in passing as we felt there was some connection with us having been in the area when the man with the bomb was found. Robert gave her a strange look and replied, 'The bomb was intended for you'. We were stunned. We had had no idea that the Forces of the Left could work in this way, i.e. that the energy of evil could manipulate people for its own ends.

We also realised that Robert kept quiet about a lot of things, trusting to our own common sense but also providing a lot more protection than we knew. He later said that he might be on the beach walking the dog and he would tune in to us to see how we were getting on. So we could be mentally influenced by the Other Side to change our plans if we did not protect ourselves adequately. In retrospect, we can remember feeling mentally confused as we kept changing our minds about where we were going to go for the day. We had even lingered in the area longer than we intended but, fortunately, had not been influenced to take the Underground.

We now had to wait until the Ring reformed itself. It seemed to us that what we were doing was both destroying and cleansing it at the same time. Each time we destroyed/unmade it, its evil vibrations would be lessened, thus purifying it. In the meantime we set about finding the shape of the crab in the streets and landmarks of London for the astrological sign of the water sign, Cancer.

Chapter 7

Red Eyes in the Night

Although Cassie had been in Salisbury for a year, she had still not found a permanent home and was 'camping' in a cramped flat with most of their furniture in storage. Moreover, it was close to a ring road <u>and</u> a roundabout, both of which we later found can be used to channel the energy of the evil Rings of Power which are still in existence at the astral levels. It was the end of September 1998 and we were still blissfully ignorant of the roles we had already begun to enact.

One morning Cassie had a flash of black in her mind's eye as she went about her daily business and then it was gone. It happened a second time during the course of the day and she wondered what it meant. That night in bed, she suddenly saw several black-cloaked figures descend upon her with fierce, glowing red eyes. She was so frightened she hid her head under the pillow to shut off the terrifying images. Not knowing what to make of it, she thought no more about it but from that day on she would wake every morning to find that her left arm had gone dead.

This had continued throughout the month of October 1998 when, at the end of that month, we made a trip to Wales to see Robert for private consultations. Robert has his own therapy business which includes crystal healing, Reiki healing and counselling. Our private sessions were on the Saturday and we were spending the night at a Bed and Breakfast so that we could attend a workshop he was giving the following day.

During Cassie's appointment she remembers the conversation turning to the story of *The Lord of the Rings* and hearing Robert telling her that she was in the role of Frodo. Unfortunately, she was 'stuck on Weathertop' and he was trying to get her off! Naturally, she was aghast. He went on to say that her shoulder had been hurting, which was true. We had both of us, unsurprisingly, read *The Lord of the Rings* not long ago since our memorable meeting in Lydney so she understood how dire was her situation. It was on Weathertop that the four hobbits, guided by Strider, were attacked by five of the dreaded Black Riders, or Nazgul, and Frodo was stabbed in the shoulder. He was now in grave danger of becoming a wraith just like them and falling wholly under the power of the Dark Lord if he did not receive healing for his wound in time.

Suddenly, she remembered her experience of a month ago when she had been attacked in her bed at night. She noticed that Robert had begun to give healing to her shoulder with a crystal, even though she had not mentioned this experience to him. It occurred to her that she had received a real stab wound that night to one of her lighter 'bodies' that surround the physical body, hence the reason for her arm going dead. He then sat to one side of her and placed the palm of his hand on the middle of her back, and looked as if he was about to put a lot of effort into the hand. At that precise moment Cassie felt warmth spread through her whole body. He explained that he was now in the role of Glorfindel who gave Frodo healing, briefly, before he and his companions reached the safety of Rivendell. At this point in the Story it says that Frodo felt a warmth come into his shoulder and travel down his arm and the pain eased as Glorfindel gives him healing, just as Cassie experienced.

Robert went on to explain that Caroline was the tall, grim Strider, who turns out to be Aragorn, the rightful heir to the throne. Without her, Cassie/Frodo would go round in circles, just as the hobbits would have done in the Story without Aragorn to guide them. Cassie commented that he, Robert, had to be Gandalf, to which he agreed but also said that he would be stepping in and out of different roles in the Story, as necessary.

He asked her where Rivendell might be and she offered some geographical places without much conviction, so that Robert eventually said that it was a 'timeless place'. When she reached it, in her role as Frodo, she would be healed of a wound to her heart. This was where he was trying to get her and where other people would appear who would make up the Fellowship of the Nine to set against the Nine Black Riders. These people would slip in and out of different roles but that hers and Caroline's roles would remain the same. It was useful he said for us to have prior knowledge of the unfolding Story having re-read *The Lord of the Rings,* since Robert first mentioned it earlier in July.

As for the wound to her heart, this must be referring to the knife wound to her shoulder. When Frodo reaches Rivendell, he receives healing from Elrond, Master of

Rivendell, who discovers that a splinter from the deadly dagger is slowly working its way inwards towards Frodo's heart.

It was important to be aware that Gollum was also out there somewhere. Gollum was the pathetic but dangerous creature who had possessed the Ring or, rather, been possessed by the evil power of the Ring for many years. To be without it was a torture to him and he was driven try and reclaim it for his own, as it was 'his Precious'. Cassie remembers feeling genuinely frightened at the thought of Gollum seeking the One Ring and therefore herself.

Chapter 8

The Olives Court Guest House

For our weekend with Robert in South Wales, Caroline had booked us into *The Olives Court Guest House,* just off the roundabout on a ring road which, as we now knew, were used to channel the evil energy of the One Ring. It was a substantial house with a large wide hall so we were surprised to be shown our bedroom on the ground floor, immediately to the left of the main entrance where you would have expected a reception room. Our bedroom didn't have a proper window but there was a narrow conservatory-like room between the window and our bedroom, which seemed a bizarre arrangement. This room was full of junk. With our heads buzzing with Robert's astounding revelations and the story of The Lord of the Rings somewhat uppermost in our minds, we both immediately thought the same thing when we noticed that we had a red, emergency exit light actually in our bedroom. Surely, this was the Eye of Mordor which appears red on the distant horizon.

As many people know, Sauron's Eye is actively seeking the One Ring, which Frodo is carrying. Its recovery is uppermost in Sauron's mind since he learnt of its rediscovery by a hobbit, a certain Bilbo Baggins, as it contains a great part of his evil power. We couldn't help noticing that there was a particularly intense spot of red in the light, slightly off-centre, which was 'looking' directly at Cassie's bed. We thought of covering it up but decided that would be a fire risk so all we could do was ignore it. We neither of us liked what appeared to be Cassie/Frodo's exposure to this red eye, particularly at night, when the Nazgul/Black Riders drew greater strength.

Nor had it escaped our attention that we were sleeping on the ground floor, just as hobbits did in their sandy holes. It occurred to us that we were re-enacting that part of the Story when Frodo and companions had reached the Inn of *The Prancing Pony* with the Black Riders in hot pursuit. Special ground floor rooms with round windows had been built just for hobbit travellers and it was these rooms that Frodo and his companions were given for the night, just like us!

They were in great danger at this point in the Story, as news of their arrival at the inn was taken by spies to the Black Riders. Soon after, two of the dreaded Nazgul turn up at the inn. It was therefore no coincidence that this B&B was close to a 'ring' road and a roundabout and it would explain the presence of the Red Eye in our bedroom for the Black Riders were directly under the control of The Eye.

Coming out of the bedroom Cassie happened to look at the picture in the hall close to our bedroom door and was stunned. It was an old photograph of a woman dressed in Victorian clothes standing in front of a home cut into a sandstone bank reminiscent of a hobbit home. She had never seen such a thing before.

It had been raining rather heavily in recent days and the landlord was having difficulty with the electricity in the house, which meant that our television kept cutting out, as well as our bedside lights and the bathroom light. Unfortunately, the red emergency light was unaffected by these vagaries and shone very brightly red when we turned off our lights to go to sleep.

We told the proprietor about our lighting problem and he was most apologetic and bustled about trying to fix the problem, talking all the while. He offered to make us sandwiches for our workshop the next day to make up for it, which we gladly accepted. Suddenly he reminded us of the bustling, talkative landlord of *The Prancing Pony*, Barliman Butterbur, who had been extremely apologetic to Frodo for failing to pass on a letter to him from Gandalf. He was also most generous to the travellers in supplying them with a pony and provisions for their onward journey!

By the end of the workshop the next day, after the initial excitement of being told about the roles we were playing had died down and we realised that a difficult task might lie ahead of us, we thought the inevitable question "why us"? We, therefore, before setting off for home at the end of the workshop, asked Robert when had we agreed to take these parts. The answer came back "A long time ago". Cassie added that she felt it had been touch and go whether or not she would be up to the job, and Robert agreed. She was referring to the clearing work we had done on ourselves over the past six years. Past life traumas, which lay in our subconscious, had been brought to our attention and we had had to deal with the ensuing emotions.[7] This coincided with her discovering the trauma of the Sacred King and how it lived on in subsequent lives buried in the subconscious mind.

Chapter 9

A Silver Ring

At the end of the workshop, Cassie suddenly remembered that she possessed a ring, which could be said to resemble the One Ring. It is a plain, quite thick, silver band but for a raised line which runs sinuously all the way around, crudely resembling the famous words inscribed all the way around the One Ring which read: 'One Ring to rule them all, One Ring to find them, One Ring to bring them all and in the darkness bind them.'

How Cassie came by it also curiously resembles the manner in which Frodo came by his Ring. It happened about a year prior to her leaving Northampton in 1998. A friend suggested they go to a crafts exhibition being held in a private house in an outlying village. One of the items which caught her eye was the silver ring just described, only the silversmith who had made it said she couldn't have that ring as it was for show, but that he could make her a similar one. Unusually, the silversmith delivered the ring, personally, in an envelope to Cassie at her home. Frodo also received his Ring in an envelope placed on the mantelpiece in his home. We were struck by the close comparison. Another thought: because the ring was specially made for her, it is unique, just like the One Ring.

Frodo was warned by Gandalf to keep Bilbo's ring safe and not to wear it, as he had begun to suspect that it could be the One Ring made by the Dark Lord himself. If it were to be recovered by its evil master, then there would be no hope for the free peoples of the West and all would fall under The Shadow, so Gandalf knew he could take no chances. Strangely, just like Frodo, Cassie hardly ever wore her ring as she found the silver tracery on the band dug into the sides of her fingers. However, she had started to wear it regularly at about the time this Story begins, and was wearing it on that fateful trip to Wales when Robert told us we were characters in the Story. She only ever thought hers to be a symbolic 'copy', although in this, she was later to discover she may have been mistaken.

Chapter 10

The Kernel of the Story

We had much to think over on the journey home across the Severn Bridge. There were too many 'proofs' for us to be able to deny the truth of what Robert had told us at our private sessions. There was the Ring, which Cassie came by so curiously, the fierce red-eyed attack by dark figures one night and subsequent pain in the shoulder as well as the 'dead' arm. Caroline's present wanderings reflected Aragorn's life in the Story. Then there was the red 'eye' in our bedroom at the guesthouse.

We quickly agreed that another talk was necessary to find out more about what was involved and to try and grasp what precisely we were doing by taking on these roles. So a month later we paid another visit to Robert having decided upon a joint sitting.

He began by telling us more about himself. For one thing, he says he has an empty mind and that he is only given information on a 'need to know' basis. In this way he lives entirely in the present. In addition to his healing practice, he also clears places of negativity, including supermarkets! Because he himself never knows what clearing he will be doing next, he stays one step ahead of the Forces of the Left. This was further confirmation that our thoughts can very quickly be picked up out of the ether by those forces. Unfortunately, he criticised us for having done so little clearing work of late – not that we had discussed the subject: he just knew. He also explained that we need to take 'Them' by surprise. If we plan t too much in advance, which is what we had been doing, 'They' can move out of an area before we have enclosed it in a circle of light which effectively traps them within that area. Our understanding is, that those evil ones are obliged / forced by the new energy to leave the lower astral level from where they feed off the negative energies that have built up over time.

To return to the story of *The Lord of the Rings*, Robert told us that we had counterparts on the Other Side, probably in physical bodies like ourselves, although he has never confirmed this and for some reason we have never asked. The more we could work out for ourselves, the better. Whenever he helps us, his opposite number is able to offer similar help to our opposites. This has meant that, throughout, Robert has only ever given us cryptic clues which, often, we could not at first understand. Only with a great deal of thought, trial and error, or with Robert eventually having to give us further clues, have we been able to go forward on this Quest.

It was an eye-opener to realise that the forces of evil are active in the world today and that we are still very much in the story of *The Lord of the Rings*. It is almost a taboo subject to talk about good and evil in stark terms, yet if we look at what is around us we can see that humanity is being manipulated so that it swings from one crisis to another to keep the energy of fear and anger flowing. In particular, we are increasingly caught up in the extreme highs and lows of the ever-growing sports industry.

The oft-repeated expression "history repeats itself" took on a more realistic tinge. In fact the balance of power is in favour of the Forces of the Left with, Robert told us, a ratio of 67% to 33%. Our aim, Robert said, was to make it 50/50. We were intrigued that he did not talk about 'vanquishing' the forces of darkness, which has always been an unquestioning article of faith of the Christian church and, therefore, of our conditioned minds.

He also pointed out that there was no linear time in the journey and if Cassie did not learn the lessons - she believes those were the words - she could find herself back on the Barrow-Downs. This was a most unpleasant prospect. The Barrow-Downs were inhabited by evil Barrow-Wights, particularly malignant spirits who haunted the barrows where the dead were laid to rest. Frodo and his party had fallen into the clutches of one of these creatures and would have perished but for Tom Bombadil.

At this same meeting, Robert suddenly started saying that he was being shown a little boy dressed like Lord Fauntleroy and that we were being told we could draw on the power of the royal line to help us. On two different occasions Robert mentioned that we could give up at any time if we wished, but for two Sagittarians, who are naturally adventurous and like a challenge, this was not an option. Matter-of-factly, but closely watching us, he said that there were two of us in case one of us should "go".

We were told that we could change the story. However, we turned out to be somewhat inexpert at knowing which parts we might change and which we might not. When we mentioned that we might like to miss out the adventures in the Mines of Moria, Robert said that this was one part of the story we had to experience.

At one time he quietly said that the 'kernel' of the Story of the Ring was the love and friendship which developed between the members of the Fellowship in the course of their Quest. A strong friendship developed between Legolas, the Elf, and Gimli, the Dwarf, which overrode the traditional mistrust between these two races. It would not be too far from the truth to say that it is just such mistrust and prejudice between nations which is still at the root of most conflicts in the world today and which makes us realise the importance of such friendship and why Robert called it the 'kernel' of the Story. Perhaps the friendship between Elf and Dwarf and their shared adventures can be described as the first 'buddy' story! Interestingly, the actors who made up the Fellowship of the Nine in the recently made film of the trilogy of *The Lord of the Rings*, also formed a strong bond amongst themselves.

The same theme is to be found in a number of popular television series - *Friends*, *Sex in the City* and also *Desperate Housewives*. The main characters draw great strength from the unwavering love and support of a diverse group of friends through all the ups and downs in their lives. Inevitably, the Dark Forces, targeted our Fellowship in the hope of disrupting the Quest.

Chapter 11

The Water Sign of The Crab

From time to time, we would dowse to see if the One Ring had reconstituted itself and was exercising its malevolent power in the affairs of Men once again. And in December, the answer came back that this was the case. The earliest date we could set aside for our first attempt at cleansing it in the element of water was 30 December 1998.

The clue we had been given was 'water in Regent's Park'. We opened the map and located the lake 'in Regent's Park. Uppermost in our minds was the idea that the astrological water sign was most likely going to be Cancer the crab. As we stared at the outline of the lake we saw to our amazement and mounting excitement that the lake was in the shape of the female reproductive organs. On the north side the lake branches out sideways, east and west, to form the arms of the fallopian tubes. Below is the womb and the water then narrows to create a long birth canal. How fitting that the womb should be located in the sign of Cancer which represents the archetypal Mother.

Excitedly, we looked for the shape of a crab in the surrounding roads and there it was, in the roads that defined the shape of the park. There was even to be seen the hard outer shell created by the main roads, and the soft, inner body of the crab is defined by an inner path which runs parallel to the 'outer' main roads. Two roads to the north gave the crab

CANCER ~ *the Crab*

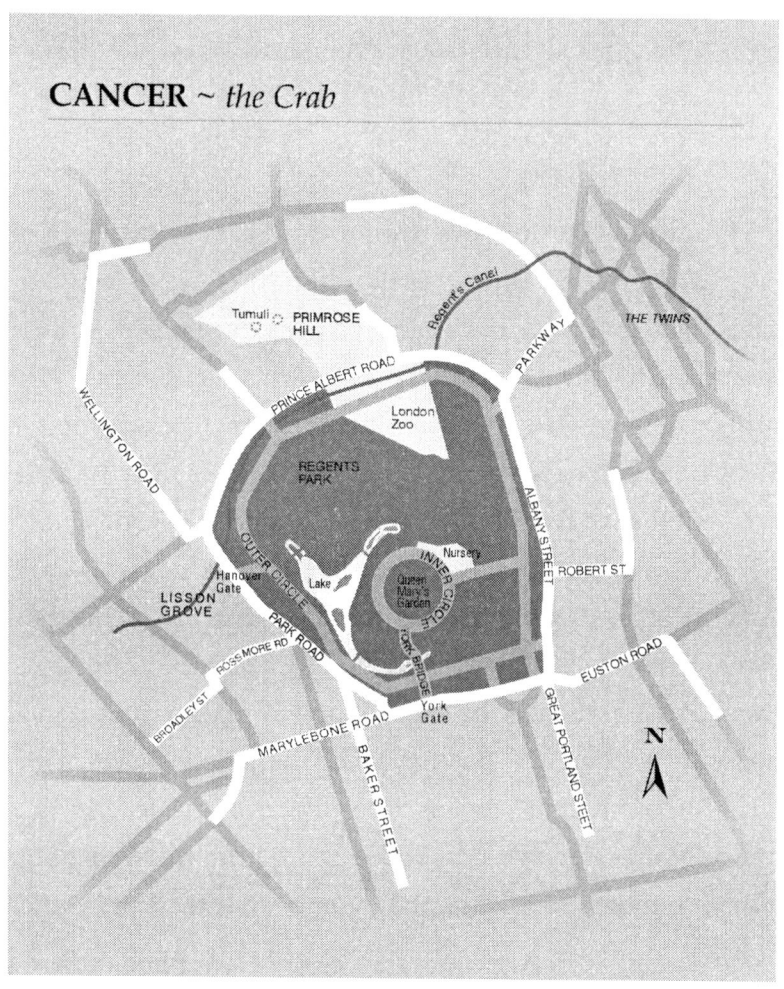

its pincers and roads to the east, south and west, its legs and eye stalks. We knew with certainty that this was the sign of Cancer and felt awed that someone at sometime had devised this.

As the site of the cleansing of the Ring in Fire had been at one of the testes, it followed that the place of power would be at one of the ovaries and, incredibly, these could be seen in the lake as small islands. We realised that it all made perfect, logical sense. Evil is the negation of life and what is more life-giving than the source of life itself – the coming together of the masculine and feminine to create new life?

The next thing was to find an energy centre where we could summon the Ring. We eventually decided on All Souls, Langham Place: it was near Regent's Park and in a relatively quiet location. It also happened to be the church at which Caroline's parents were married. First we had to clear the church of any negativity. We realised that the best way to achieve all this in an afternoon on an overcast day in December, was to go by cab, which we duly did and were set down without incident at All Souls. As we had suspected, this beautiful Wren church with its rounded, feminine entrance was locked as are, sadly, a great number of London churches today. However, we walked round the side and found a quiet corner. It was Cassie's turn to call the Ring. She felt a tingling in the palm of her hand which told us that the Ring was present there, if not visible, and the Ring was once again tipped into the handkerchief, wrapped up and put in the pocket of her coat. We then hailed another cab, which took us to Hanover Gate, the nearest entrance to the north end of the lake and the two little islands.

We began walking across the north end of the lake towards a bridge where we hoped we would see a way to get down to the water's edge to get close to the little island/ovary on the East side. Aware of the need for vigilance, Caroline's attention was drawn to a man with two large dogs walking towards us. As he drew level he met her gaze and proceeded to give her a look of pure hatred the like of which she has never witnessed in her entire life. Her jaw dropped; what had she done to this man? She told Cassie who thought she must be imagining it, but when she turned to see what he was doing, he had also stopped and was looking back at us, but this time he appeared to be avoiding Caroline's gaze. We continued on to the bridge. Off to the left at the side of a small building seemed hopeful, but we found the way barred and had to retrace our steps. As we did so, we caught sight of the same man who had turned back and was now quite definitely watching our movements. We enveloped him in Light as the best way we could think of to protect ourselves. Later we were to learn that there is nothing the Other Side like so much as Light! They then riposte with black energy, thereby perpetuating the battle between Good and Evil. Without Light they would not have a target. The thing to be is neutral, or grey, like Gandalf the Grey: nor must you feel any fear. Only then can evil find no point of entry. When clearing sites Robert would say that people who are accustomed to the dark find the light too dazzling and why don't we use neutral energy in place of light.

We didn't know this at the time but when Caroline later recounted this to Robert, he gave his usual laugh. He told us that the man we had encountered was a Viking and that he and the other Vikings were angry with us. Then we remembered that we had just done a lot of clearing work in East Anglia where, historically, many Vikings had settled. They were still there, at the lower astral dimension, and did not take kindly to being dislodged.

A ghost is one thing but a fully physical person manifesting themselves is quite another. When we were making revisions to Ring Quest we realised that we did not understand how this was possible. What process was enabling this man to materialise? So we decided to see if Robert could elucidate and this is the e-mail he sent in reply:

> "some spirits who have intense energy and a very strong belief system can over-ride the normal limits or boundaries of inter- dimensional travel or movement - for one such as the Viking, there would have to be a number of living people here at this level for him to have enough energy to materialise in the physical. There are a small number of beings who do this, usually for their own gain, proper Time Lords - Avatars etc.
> Some spirits retain their evil ways and it is our duty to be of sufficient brightness to help them. Evil only exists within human consciousness or the levels that humans attain to i.e. spirit form."

When we next saw him he asked if what he had sent had been helpful and that a lot more could be said on the subject. For the purposes of this book, though, he must have understood that we needed more of a sound bite than a treatise.

We leaned over the bridge again to get a better look at the other ovary, this time to the West. We noticed a spot close to the water's edge beneath some willow trees, which seemed accessible from the path running down that side. This was going to be the closest we could get to the island so we walked back along the path retracing our steps.

Cancer, being a feminine sign, we could expect to find evidence of the Goddess, and we were not disappointed. Gazing down from the bridge, we saw a pair of beautiful swans unlike any we had seen before with white bodies, a red protuberance on their beaks and black necks - the colours of the Triple Goddess in her three aspects of maid, mother and wise woman. Making our way to the willows and taking care not to slip, as the ground was rather wet and sloping, we threw the Ring into the lake asking the generative Waters of Life in the womb of our Mother to cleanse and revitalise it.

We both had a deep feeling of satisfaction at having completed our task and we looked forward to a leisurely walk south through the park alongside the lake. The sun was now shining and it seemed almost like spring. Signs of the Goddess were everywhere. There was a children's playground nearby and the crescent moon on top of the golden dome of the Mosque shone in the sun. Winfield House, home to the American Ambassador, lay to the north: the United States is a sun-sign Cancer country, Nanny/Mother to the world, and we remembered that London Zoo is in the park - the Goddess is Mistress of the Animals. As we wandered back past the lake we passed Queen Mary's Rose Garden, Mary, the mother of Jesus, being the Goddess of the Piscean Age, and the rose her emblem. A squirrel ran towards us and ate an apricot and some bread from our hands. The lake was teeming with waterfowl already paired for spring and a fresh round of new life. So ended our second cleansing of the Ring.

Caroline later realised a continuing royal theme in our Quest which had begun with our discovery of the outline of the Lion and the Star of David/Elendil and been reinforced with references to kingship at the Chapel of the Royal Hospital in Chelsea. We had left the park at York Gate having entered at the Hanover Gate. She felt it symbolised the demise of the Stuarts in the figure of the Duke of York, who had become James II (he literally fled his Kingdom throwing the Royal Seal into the Thames in his haste to reach France and safety) and the entering in of a new dynasty: the House of Hanover.

Just as we began revisions on this chapter Cassie happened to look at a map of London 'on-line' which only showed the major roads. As she looked at Regent's Park, the names of the main roads which encircle the park therefore jumped out. To the North is Albert Road, to the South is Marylebone and to the East is Albany Street. The message was that the opposites, masculine and feminine, come together at this park and that it is a royal coupling. Albert was the Prince Consort of Queen Victoria and Mary is a name much connected with royalty, not least because she was the mother of Jesus who was of the Royal Line of David. Researchers, tracing the descendants of that Royal Line who came to Europe in the book *The Holy Blood and The Holy Grail*, found that it ran through the line of the Dukes of Albany – the name on the East side of the park.

We also suddenly realised the significance of the name of the park itself – Regent – a word that can be either male or female. In esoteric books the One, in origin, is neither masculine nor feminine.

At the same time she realised that the path known as the Inner Circle and a small wriggly path leading into the circle called York Bridge, represented a sperm. The fact that it is huge and of similar proportions as the lake 'womb' must be showing us that the role of the masculine is of equal importance as the feminine in the act of creation. The second discovery confirmed the first. Here, anchored at the gross physical is the energy of the opposites coming together in love and harmony to create new life. We simply had not noticed this until now, nine years later because the sperm's tail had been concealed by a word written across it on the map we consulted at that time. The royal theme was to continue in the outline of the Divine Twins in the astrological sign of Gemini.

Chapter 12

New Surroundings and the Number 44

At our last meeting with Robert at the end of October, he had told Cassie that her present living circumstances had put her in one of the most perilous places in the Story – on the hill called Weathertop. She had to move and in March 1999 she found a house on the top of a hill, where it was quiet and leafy and outside the ring road. It was also a sufficient distance from the nearest roundabout,.

The number of the house was 44, as had been the number of her previous house in Northampton. A few weeks later, quite by chance, she bought a car whose model number was 440. We suddenly became aware how Cassie was being dogged by the number 44 and wondered why. We found out from Robert that it means 'death and destruction' which, if you think about it, was the aim of Frodo's quest: to bring about the death and destruction of Sauron and his mighty Evil Empire. But this happy outcome was by no means certain. Indeed, the Quest was looked upon as a desperate venture with little chance of success. The danger was very great that Frodo and Samwise would be captured by the Enemy. The Ring of Power would then be used to bring about the 'death and destruction' of the peoples of the West.

Fascinating correspondences between real life and the story in the Lord of the Rings continued. It turned out that Cassie's new landlord was a farmer who was unusually small with curly brown hair: in short, he had to be a hobbit. Additional clues pointed to the fact that he was in the role of Bilbo Baggins. His surname, Riddle, reminded us of the terrifying riddling game Bilbo played with Gollum in the dark roots of the mountain in Tolkien's *The Hobbit*, which was a precursor to *The Lord of the Rings*. This is a great moment in the history of The Ring as it was at that moment that the Ring chose to change hands and be picked up by Bilbo so as to come into the light of day and set in train the momentous events in the Story.

Mr Riddle was a bachelor, just like Bilbo, and also like Bilbo, he had a favourite nephew (Frodo had been Bilbo's favourite nephew and he had made him his heir, leaving him Bag End, his grand hobbit hole). Indeed, so fond was Mr Riddle of his own nephew that he had brought him a house to live in during his years at university. This money had now been reinvested in a property in Salisbury to let to none other than Cassie/Frodo. It seemed that he was being Bilbo Baggins to Cassie's Frodo in providing a roof over her head, just as Bilbo had done.

As Cassie began to explore this new part of town she came across a very strange antique/junk shop in a side street, which she became fond of visiting, picking up items for the new house and talking to the owner. However, it was the shop keeper's name which made Cassie's jaw drop: his name was Bill Biggins which is remarkably close to Bilbo Baggins. Just like Bag End, you could say his shop was full of 'mathoms' as hobbits called them, or useless items! Perhaps

Mr Biggins's eccentricity is also a further comparison with Mr Baggins who was thought eccentric by his fellow hobbits.

But perhaps the single most dramatic feature, which dominates Salisbury, is the Cathedral with its tall spire. Salisbury is a small, medieval, market town. Almost every vista shows the beautiful spire on the sky line. Because of its height, a red light is set on its pinnacle to alert overhead aircraft coming in to land at nearby Boscombe Down airfield. There was little doubt in our minds that the red light also represents the Eye of Sauron. This was set in the topmost part of the Black Tower of Mordor from where it kept a ceaseless vigilance over the affairs of Men.

Some years later, we remembered that the Cathedral spire, the tallest in England, is 404 feet making the number 44 again, so attracting the energy of 'death and destruction'. Was this mere coincidence? We thought not. It seemed that for the purposes of our Quest, the Cathedral represents the Black Tower of the Dark Lord. Quite simply, its symbolic fall would spell the total destruction of Sauron's Empire, as it was driven and controlled by the One Evil Will set in that Tower.

It was not long after moving into her new home that Cassie was given an insight into the nature of the silver Ring she had so curiously acquired. She was having a cup of coffee with a neighbour, who admitted that she was somewhat psychic and who made the observation that Cassie's ring was tingling with energy. The remark caused Cassie to think of a conversation she had had with Robert not long ago.

Concerning her housing problems at the time, he had suggested, to her surprise and confusion, "Why don't you use your Ring"? But she had thought better of it, remembering that in the original Story this might have helped the Other Side to locate the Ring and come after it. So she had not done so. Her neighbour's comment confirmed that she was right not to have used the Ring, or was she? How were we to reconcile the One Ring of Power, which existed only at the etheric, with the silver replica which now appeared to be imbued with power as well? We were not to work this conundrum out for some years.

It must be said here that neither of us is psychic. When we commented on this to Robert he said that it was too dangerous for us to be psychic in that way as we could very easily be led to our deaths. This had already nearly happened merely through mind suggestion, which resulted in our changing our plans for a day's outing in London with Cassie's daughters. But we did have protection in this Quest. We had the equivalent of Frodo's corselet of mithril rings and precious gems, and Aragorn was watched over from afar by Arwen, daughter of Elrond, the Master of Rivendell, to whom he was betrothed.

Chapter 13

The Air Sign of the Twins

For some time, we knew that the next sign would be the Air sign Gemini, known as the Twins. We, therefore, began looking for things connected to communication of all kinds, which is the main characteristic of that sign and includes talking, travel, education, journalism, as well as commerce and youth. Our attention was drawn to Camden Town, a young place with a market buzzing with energy. Looking at the roads we thought we could make out two almost identical shapes, side by side. The more we looked, the more convinced we became. One of the oblong shapes is clearly feminine as it is curvy and even goes in at the 'waist', whilst the other is straight-sided. Within the two outlines are a library, a health centre, Parcel Force, MTV Studios and the Royal Veterinary College. It is interesting that the Veterinary College lies within the female twin, as animals come under the protection of her Mother, the Queen, who is the Goddess's representative. Then to our wonder we noted that the Regent's Canal, which once transported goods on barges, runs through both figures. This combines the Geminian qualities of travel and commerce, as well as demonstrating the Royal Line coming from their Mother.

We noticed that the Twins lie very close to the sign of Cancer, their mother, and that the birth canal of the lake points in their direction as well. For the cleansing of

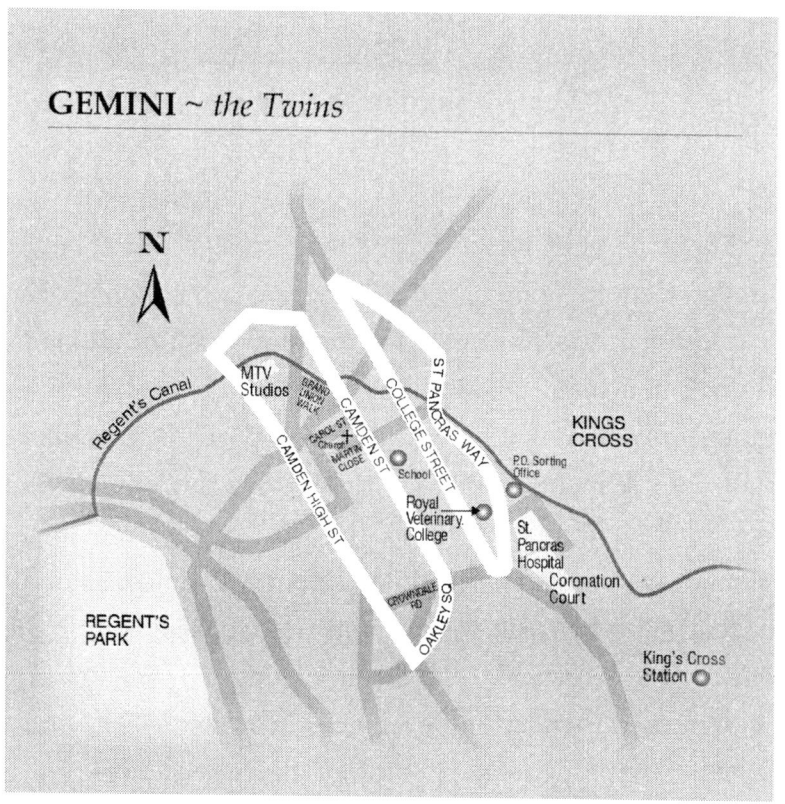

the Ring in Air we had chosen to go to the site of St Paul's Cathedral to fetch the Ring, as neither of us had been to that magnificent building for some time. The date was Sunday, 14 February 1999. As usual we did our protection: grounding and balancing ourselves using the daisy. We then visualise a circle of protection around us, which has to be renewed from time to time, particularly after crossing a threshold, such as entering or leaving a building or passing beneath a bridge.

The Cathedral was full of people milling around, as might be expected, but we managed to find a quiet spot and quietly summoned the Ring into the palm of the hand. We then took a cab and were dropped off in Camden at the intersection to the three straight highways, which form part of the outline of the Twins whose roads run north and south.

We had found the energy site quite easily because there were the most extraordinary clues. On either side of a green area, as shown on the map, were two streets. The one to the north was called Carol Street and the one to the south, Martin Close: in other words, Cassie's maiden name and Caroline's Christian name. Caroline was actually christened Carol as the date given for her birth was Christmas Day. It appears that the Universe already knew that we would be carrying out this quest at the energy point between the two streets and the names were there to guide us to the right spot. Many have heard the statement that there is no such thing as Time and here is the proof! Recently, there had been a programme on television demonstrating this where grid lines in space fold back on themselves showing that the present and future are the same and that there is no such thing as linear time. Other sources say that linear time was given to us to help us get back to God, as we have become separated from the true Reality.

Unfortunately, when Caroline telephoned Robert and told him that we had found the exact sites for cleansing the Ring in the signs of Gemini and Taurus, he told her that the Other Side had immediately taken it. This was because she had failed to secure the area for the forces of Light by putting her hand on the map with the purpose of protecting it. We therefore had to look elsewhere and eventually chose from the map a nearby school. However, when we reached it the atmosphere around it was so flat that we felt very disinclined to go in and wandered on down the road until we saw a recreation ground with benches. We decided to go in and ponder what to do next. After a while we noticed a War Memorial Cross and thought that would be as good a spot as any but, as we approached, we saw a man nearby so we turned away. It was then that we saw we were in what had been an old churchyard. There were tombstones round the edge of the grounds and evidence of a ruined church in the middle. Part of the ruined walls was curved and was obviously the remains of the chancel, which was shaded by a thorn tree. This was our site: a place of power, which had been enclosed and was once again open to the air, as was appropriate for the Air Sign, Gemini. Without hesitation, as we were always aware that the Other Side were trying to prevent us, we stood under the thorn tree and threw the Ring into the air asking for it to be cleansed in that element. We also remembered to send the energy down the lines to cleanse the other Rings of Power around the world. This time we did not feel too jubilant, as we weren't absolutely certain we had found the right location.

As soon as we arrived back at the house we took out the map and saw that the recreation ground was, in fact, the very spot between Carol Street and St. Martin's Close, after all, and Robert confirmed that we had been in exactly the right place at exactly the right time. Something must have happened to secure it for the forces of Light. A possible explanation is that, knowing our intention was to go elsewhere, the Forces of the

Left had left the site unguarded. Being new to the area, we had stumbled unwittingly upon the original site. Caroline told Robert that we had kept an eye open for any suspicious characters but had not seen anything untoward. He laughed and said that, on the contrary, we had been followed all the way!

When revising the above part of the book some years later, we had one of those synchronicities. Caroline was in a shop buying cakes to bring over to Cassie's house for morning coffee. What should she see but female identical twins, each with a child of the same age in a push chair.

This time round we were also on the look out for connections with royalty within the outlines of the pair. First off, the road running down one side of the female twin is called Royal College Street. There is a B road, in yellow running East West, which joins the twins like a golden umbilical cord and it is called Crowndale Road. The curving road forming the bottom of the male twin's outline is called Oakley Square and as everyone knows, the oak is connected with the King and lives on in pub signs called *The Royal Oak* often showing the head of the future King Charles II who hid in the branches of the tree. Perhaps you could make a case for the significance of the road forming one side of the male twin, which is Camden High Street. This king is the 'High' King, just like Aragorn. Also, they are high in the sense of being spiritually higher than the people in their care, just as were the King Elessar (Aragorn) and Queen Arwen.

We did not much like King's Cross Station being just to the East of the Royal Twins as we realised it was telling us how the King came to be a victim who was also crucified (he was put to death in many different ways) in the Cult of human sacrifice.

It seems to us that two royal couples are being suggested in the astrological signs – our Heavenly Father and Mother, as represented by the Lion and the Crab, and the earthly King and Queen, The Twins, who are the son and daughter of the Father/Mother God who are their representatives on earth.

Chapter 14

Enemies

On 10 May 1999, just two months after Cassie had moved to her new home, Robert and a number of friends came down to Salisbury as Robert had agreed to give a talk on crystal healing at The Salisbury Homeopathy Centre on the Sunday, with private consultations on the Saturday afternoon. It was over this weekend that Robert put forward an extraordinary idea.

Our friends from across the River Severn, Enid, Julia and Clarissa, plus ourselves and Robert, were having a cup of tea after the private sittings on the Saturday afternoon when Robert again brought up the subject of The Lord of the Rings. He offered Enid, Julia and Clarissa the opportunity to participate and they were happy to do so. He then said "What would you think of keeping the Ring? What if you could use it for Good this time round and change the Story?" This was yet a new slant on the idea of cleansing the Ring, which had not entered our heads. We were all speechless as the idea slowly began to filter through.

Leaving this new idea with us he went on to say that one of the Rings of Power was hovering over the city of Salisbury and was drawing the Other Side to the area. They were massing on the borders. Saruman was based at Old Sarum to the north (in the Story the orcs called him '*Old* Man'), Sauron was at the hill fort at Grovely Woods to the west - he pointed to the woods on an Ordnance Survey Map saying they made the shape of a crocodile advancing on Salisbury. Morganic, as in Morgan Le Fey (King Arthur's sister), energy was coming from the south and Merlin energy from the south west. They were all bent on snatching the Ring for themselves.

In one breath Robert was suggesting that Merlin was not the force for good that we have been led to believe, and that Morgan Le Fey, the legendary King Arthur's sister, was not just a mythical figure and was out for power for herself. We were to learn more about Merlin later. However, we were able to understand the 'Morganic energy' and its source because of the research that Cassie had been doing on the pagan cults of the Goddess and Sacred King. Morgan Le Fey was one of the cruel Queens of those times who scorned men. She was now attempting to recover her former, absolute power by drawing on a corrupted feminine energy of that forgotten period of history. As Robert has said, nothing ever goes, it is still being recycled out there close to the dense physical, layer upon layer.

Caroline and Cassie, Robert told us cheerfully, were quite oblivious of all these different negative energies being drawn to Salisbury. Cassie had been lulled into a false sense of security by the Other Side. She had been imagining that she was safely in the Shire surrounded by comforting hobbits whom she kept meeting (this was true!), whereas she was really only approaching the Fords of Bruinen – where all nine Black Riders were lying in wait for her - and was completely unprotected.

Hence, perhaps, the timely visit of our friends. As we sat drinking our tea we realised we each represented a member of Frodo's party who were trying to reach Rivendell, and without whose help at the Fords, Frodo would not have won through. Robert was Glorfindel, as he had told us before, Enid, Julia and Clarissa were variously, Samwise, Pippin and Merry, and Caroline was Aragorn. So, just as the Other Side can use the negative energy for their purposes, the forces of Good can use the good energy in the Story to ensure that people of good intent appear at need.

Robert then startled us all by saying that this Ring had taken physical form and he pointed to a pink dot on the local map, which was the rail station and said, "It is south of that, on or near a wall."

Chapter 15

A Black Ring on an Island

The next day, Monday, the others having all gone home, we decided that we should take action sooner rather than later, before the Other Side were able to manipulate events at the physical level so as to acquire the Ring of Power in Salisbury. To be truthful, we felt somewhat fainthearted as we set off in Cassie's car, wondering how on earth we were going to find a Ring, what kind of ring it was going to be and how big. We just thought we had better give it a try.

We decided to make straight for the station down Fisherton Street, but Cassie missed the turning and we found ourselves driving along Mill Road to the south, where we passed on our left the river Nadder. Caroline noticed a road sign saying 'Fisherton Island'. We continued on to the station, both, curiously, (we subsequently discovered) with an idea of eliminating the area surrounding it rather than with the hope of discovery. We did, in fact, draw a blank and then remembered that Robert had said that it was near water and Caroline suggested that we try the island we had just passed.

We returned to the sign and drove over the little bridge onto the island. There was a single road with pretty houses on the one side backing onto a dyke in the water meadows and a stretch of the Nadder on the other edged with rich spring vegetation. Parking the car at the end, we wandered back up the road towards the bridge, taking in glimpses of the meadows between the houses and thinking what a peaceful place it would be to live. It could have been any lovely spring day with two people chatting away with nothing in view but a pleasant day out.

We reached the bridge and looked carefully along the top of the wall, rather late in the day remembering that we should ask the Ring to show itself to us, which we did. The gardens on the opposite side of the river were rather beautiful, and Cassie walked a little way down the bank to get a better look. We were both totally unconcerned that we hadn't yet found the Ring but suddenly, as we turned to walk back, Cassie said, 'There it is', and picked something up off the ground, quickly showed it to me, and put it in her pocket. After we had both got over our initial fear of this object, we had a closer look. It was a small, black, rubber ring the size of a conventional ring with white paint on about a quarter of the surface. It was, in fact, a rubber washer and in no way a thing of beauty, but we both knew that this was what we were looking for.

On our return to the house Caroline rang Robert and told him that we'd got it, but weren't sure what to do with it. He laughed and said, 'Put it somewhere safe'. Caroline asked him whether we could start using it for good but he said that this would come later.

We looked around for a suitable receptacle and Cassie suggested a largish Middle-Eastern cigarette box, but Caroline's eye fell on a small sandalwood box, which had been in Cassie's possession for at least the last thirteen years but she could never remember how she had acquired it. It had beautiful markings all round the sides and on the top which consisted of an inlaid ring of ivory. Inside the box was a further lid with a metal ring and then four compartments.

Caroline immediately remembered that a few days before, when looking for something to read, she had pulled out a book entitled *Magic Symbols of the World*. There were shown the same intricate patterns and heavily reinforced borders on cloth, boxes, etc., designed to protect and ward off evil influences. Cassie had never been able to fathom what she could keep in the box. It didn't occur to her that it was specifically for rings. Now, however, she realised that this was its purpose and that it was the perfect place for the Ring. The numerology was also right and seemed designed to keep the Ring in physical manifestation. The box had four sides and there were four compartments. Four is the number of this physical planet.

Despite the above, we began to feel apprehensive that we might be adversely affected by the energy from the Ring and Cassie suggested that we should put a small amethyst cluster on the top remembering that Robert had told us it stopped the hypnotic, circular emanations from the TV screen. By putting it on the box, it would doubtless have the same effect on the Ring.

That night Cassie remembered a curious incident on Sunday, two days before, when, as everyone was taking their leave, Robert had pressed into her hand the amethyst cluster which lay on top of her television set. She put it back and a few minutes later he once again put it into her hand saying, 'I keep picking this up.' Earlier on he had put his glass down on top of Cassie's inlaid, Middle-Eastern box, which was on the chimney piece next to the small box. Seeing that Cassie looked rather horrified, he had made an amused, rueful expression as he lifted it off. Both of these actions now appeared significant. The fact that he went to such trouble suggests that it was very important to prevent the energy of the Ring emanating outward and that we must not underestimate the power of this object. The effect of the amethyst cluster also disguises the whereabouts of the Ring so that the Other Side are unable to locate it.

When we saw Robert again at the beginning of June he said that by imprisoning and neutralising the evil energy of the Ring we had protected the area around the city as far as Avebury, but that the Ring itself might be gone the following weekend. This was because there was to be a large gathering of people north of the city interested in crop circles. He asked us if we had ensured that the protective qualities of the amethyst crystals were all round the box including underneath, and we had to admit that we hadn't. We quickly proceeded to do this. Presumably the Ring could have used the energies of this gathering to escape.

A curious coincidence has just occurred as we make revisions to this chapter in September of 2006. Cassie went round to visit a friend who lives close to Fisherton Island where we found the physical Ring of Power all those years ago. Her friend asked if she had been to the special Open Day of the churchyard of the former St Clement's Church which is not normally open to the public and to which Cassie replied she hadn't. Her friend pointed across the road in the direction of Fisherton Island to a darkly wooded area, which Cassie had always thought formed the back gardens of the houses along the street. The church had been dismantled in 1850 as it had become too small for the expanding population.

When a person goes to some pains to give us information our attention is often being drawn to something we need to know. (This goes for everyone and is one of the ways the universal consciousness communicates with us but so often we don't notice). Looking at the print made in 1834 of the former church Cassie noticed that the church stood on a small 'mump' or gentle mound: in other words, it was sited on an energy centre which happened to be extraordinarily close – say 100 yards - to where we found the black ring seven years ago.

It all fell into place. This was a polluted energy site to which the evil energy of the etheric Ring of Power had been drawn. Furthermore, about the time of our finding the Ring seven years' ago, a mini-roundabout was created at the entrance to Fisherton Island and therefore close to the energy centre. Sure enough, when we dowsed, it had been a site of former sacrifice of the King and there were souls there who needed help in releasing themselves.

Chapter 16

Good and Evil

In talking about the Ring of Power and the forces of Good and Bad over the weekend in Salisbury in May, we were naturally thinking along the traditional Christian view of Good versus Evil, so we were caught off balance when Robert said carefully: 'What would you say if I were to ask you to think of Good and Evil as One', and as he said this he slowly brought the palms of his hands together. It seemed an entirely novel idea. He went on to say that you cannot separate light from dark, or good from evil. Where one is present, the other will be also. If we can embrace them both, balance and harmony would be ours. Certainly, we could appreciate that in this world our 'reality' is one of duality. To comprehend an abstract concept such as 'Good' or 'Light' or 'God' we have to create its opposite. But at the level of the Absolute, All is One. Shortly afterwards, Caroline and Robert happened to wander into the garden and walk over to the guinea pigs belonging to Cassie's daughters. Caroline picked out the black and white one and Robert asked her what her name was to which Caroline replied, "Twinkle". It was only the following day that the thought came to her that she had literally embraced the idea of black and white. Furthermore, in the word "Twinkle", Light and Darkness alternate as in a twinkling star.

As Caroline typed the above sentence the first time, the words spaced themselves out, firstly, with 'Light' at the beginning of the line, then nothing until the last word 'and', then the word 'Darkness' came immediately below 'Light'. Later, when she had made a few alterations to a paragraph above, these two words spaced themselves out with several spaces in between each word, and no amount of fiddling with the Word Processor would change it. Caroline thought about this for a while and then it suddenly came to her. The first instance showed that Light and Darkness are two sides of the one coin and the second had the effect of a twinkling star alternating evenly spaced black print and white paper.

At the time it was a completely new idea, at least it was for us. However, since then, others have begun to say the same thing. When one person gets an original thought, four or five others will also pick it up as it has entered the sea of consciousness, of which we all partake. There is a service held in Salisbury Cathedral, called 'Darkness into Light', which Cassie went to for the first time a couple of years later. She was struck by the fact that the service begins with the whole of the Cathedral being plunged into darkness. Gradually, hundreds of flickering candles are lit. It was a most profound experience and she could tell that everyone there felt the same way. It was demonstrating an awareness of the dark, which seemed quite new. For the most part, Christian teaching has dwelt on the light, whilst the dark has been something to be feared, suppressed, or conquered. We are told in *The Lord of the Rings* that the dark was not evil in the beginning but evil appropriated it for its own use. The darkness in the Cathedral was peaceful and gentle and everyone there fell silent, awed by its beauty in that magnificent setting.

At the time of going to press in May 2007 Cassie saw, coincidentally for the first time, two films in quick succession, which seemed to prove the statement that Good and Evil are One. The first was *The Firm* (shown on television) where it becomes evident that there is not a lot of difference between the good and the bad guys. Also, it could so clearly be seen that Evil's shadow self is Good, and Good's shadow is Evil. The outcome is unexpected by conventional standards, as the hero rejects coming down on the side of either Good or Evil. Instead, he blends the energies of both and wins back his freedom. The story reminded us of Robert's image of a coin which lies immovable when placed on one side or the other but when set on its rim, i.e. a blend of the two sides, rolls freely.

Three days later she happened to put on the video *L.A. Confidential*. Here, it was plain for all to see that the tactics of the Los Angeles Police Department are identical to those of the gangsters. In fact, the Chief of Police is planning on becoming the next Mafia boss! Again, the outcome is not what you might expect. The evil goings on within the Police Force are brought into the light of day and noted. Instead of revealing all to the press, the remaining Police hierarchy choose to harmonise those opposites of Good and Evil so as to maintain the morale of the people of Los

Angeles and their belief in the goodness of their Police Force.

These dynamics are to be found in *The Lord of The Rings* – Sauron the Black (he only stole the black horses belonging to The Riders of the great plains), Saruman the White and Gandalf the Grey. Like the Chief of the Los Angeles Police in the film, Saruman succumbed wholly to evil. But Gandalf, being grey, could not be thrown off balance. There is a beautiful description in the story when the Prince Faramir and Eowyn, daughter of Queens, stand on the walls of the White City. A wind starts to blow and their hair, fair and dark, flows out and mingles in the air.

Another case in point showing that Good and Evil are indivisible, is the problem in Iraq. When America and her allies went into that country proclaiming to be the Forces of Good come to liberate the people, they acted as a magnet for the opposing forces of anarchy and terror.

Chapter 17

Gandalf Rescued

We continued to mirror the events of the Story. One sunny morning in June Cassie was hanging out the washing when in a clear blue sky she thought she could make out the shape of an eagle in the distance. Living on a hill she had a large area of sky as her view from the washing line. The more she looked at it the more convinced she became. It was most definitely an eagle but she did not link it to an episode in the Quest. When she mentioned it to Robert he grew very upset that she had been unable to connect it to the Story and that it was vital that we should do so. It was only then that we fully understood the importance of consciously linking with the events unfolding at that other dimension in order to bring them into the present and clear them from that level. Fortunately, she had done a rough pencil sketch in her diary and realised that from the angle of the wings, the eagle was not gliding, but carrying a heavy weight. It had to be the eagle who rescued Gandalf from the pinnacle of the tower of Isengard where he had been imprisoned by Saruman who was at last revealed as a traitor. Saruman was the head of the White Council of which Gandalf was a member. The eagle, by good fortune had come seeking him to pass on news. It was a crucial point in the Story to mark for, without his rescue, Gandalf would not have been able to hive off four of the Nine Black Riders pursuing Frodo and friends. Thanks to Gandalf, therefore, on that fateful night on Weathertop hill, there were five and not nine of the Black Riders lying in wait for Aragorn and the hobbits. No wonder Robert had been upset.

With the benefit of hindsight, it seems to us that Robert has the ability to know what is going on in those parallel universes and he is able to help the way it interacts with or overlaps our dimension in such a way that we, in our bodies of clay, can notice - hence a cloud in the shape of an eagle. Our understanding is that Robert also has to work within certain restrictions.

Chapter 18

A Meeting in the Wye Valley

A series of meetings began to take place over the next five months in the Wye Valley, June to October, which constituted the Council of Elrond in the Story.

This momentous meeting in the Story saw the representatives of the free peoples of the West gathered at Rivendell, as if by chance, but clearly guided there by a higher purpose, for they were to form The Fellowship of the Ring. Gimli was to represent the Dwarves, Legolas the Elves, Boromir the Men of Gondor, Frodo, Samwise, Merry and Pippin were the Hobbits and Aragorn of the Dunedain – Numenorean stock unadulterated by intermarriage with lesser men and also of the royal line. Finally, there was Gandalf the Wizard.

The Council's aim was to decide what course of action those peoples should take for the safety of their realms against the massing of vast military forces by Sauron and his evil allies in the East, in clear preparation for open war against the West. At the meeting, the Council was to learn the history of the Ring of the Dark Lord going back in time, how it came into Bilbo's possession, who then passed it on to Frodo, and finally, of Frodo's flight from The Shire, pursued by none other than the dread servants of Sauron, the Nine Ring Lords or Black Riders, who had, once again, grown in power and terror.

The first of these meetings was on 6 June 1999, at a house in the Wye Valley, which at that particular moment represented Rivendell. As usual, it was one of Robert's talks on self-awareness, which had been advertised in various places. There was a good attendance and included people we were meeting for the first time. It was a gloriously sunny day with blue sky and puffy white clouds.

Robert told the meeting that the battle between "good" and "bad" is going on around the world and where each of us lives. It is on many levels. *The Lord of the Rings* puts it into perspective and the writings of Paulo Coelho are also useful guidelines for our actions. There were six more people at this meeting who were hearing about the re-enacting and earthing of the Story of *The Lord of the Rings* for the first time. He told the meeting that he was playing the role of Gandalf; Julia that of Elrond, Master of Rivendell, who had been like a father to Aragorn; Cassie, Frodo the Ringbearer and Caroline, Strider/Aragorn. Other roles would be given at further meetings.

Cassie talked about the Sacred Kings and said that they are still trapped at the astral level unless someone releases them. The balance between male and female is still not equal. The pendulum has now swung too far to the feminine and men are becoming uncertain of their role. This time round we have to find the balance, the still point in the middle. Robert asked if we could revitalise the Sacred Kings and bring in their masculine energy so that we can have balance.

Craig, one of the people who had been coming to Robert's workshops and was part of the Quest, had some very useful information about Gandalf which he had obtained from the internet and which he read out to us. Gandalf apparently had a twin, Gandolf, and they were separated at birth. This is why Gandalf sometimes appeared to be in two places at once. Robert said that if Gandalf and Gandolf had been acknowledged as one, *The Lord of the Rings* would have finished in a better way and Gandalf would not have had to go to the Grey Havens. However, one of them had a fear of the Ring. Robert said that if he had been Gandalf in real life, he would have played with the Ring, as it would not have affected him (just as Tom Bombadil did in the original story.)

Robert spoke of the need to find the twenty Rings, which are at large, deal with them and make them safe so that they can do no harm. We had already dealt with one, which we had found on Fisherton Island in Salisbury. The twenty rings had been given out by Sauron to the different peoples of Middle Earth so as to bring them under his control, once they had been reduced over time to wraiths so that they lived a ghastly half-life without end. But the three Elven Rings were now in great danger of being exposed to the Eye of Sauron. If the One ruling Ring, which had so recently come to light, were ever to be recovered by Sauron, then the three Elven rings and their holders would be revealed to him and come under his power. The year 2000 has three rings, the rings of the Elven-Kings: Gandalf's ring was Narya the Great, the Ring of Elrond, Vilya, and

Nenya was Galadriel's ring. In this year help from these three rings ceases.

Each of us is a holistic ring: body, mind and spirit. If we put all the rings together we form a greater whole. We are part of the collective life force. We are links and we should link with others to give them help. The difference between the Spirit and the Soul is that the spirit remains bright and spotless but that the light of the Soul dims as it carries our accumulated experiences in life. Thus the link between the two can weaken.

We need to clear sites permanently. We were shocked to learn that the Sacred Kings we had been releasing over many years, or so we thought, came and settled right back. We protested that at least they had been healed and were no longer in agony. Every King had to swear an oath to his Liege Lord, who was the outgoing King, to protect the land. Because of this, these men had felt obliged to return to the earth to fulfil their oath. In future, we should ask the Kings to ask their Liege Lords, who had been sacrificed at the same site, to be released from this oath, then, when clearing sites, we would feel the difference.

The clearing work that we do goes back in time to the story of the Ring. An insight into Robert's rationale came when he said that we are at a unique point in history where the past can be compacted into the present and we can put history right and correct the early blunders.

Another part of the Story was earthed at this meeting. Robert referred to Julia and her husband as being in the roles of Goldberry and Tom Bombadil at this particular moment, as they were our hosts for the day. Frodo and his companions were offered hospitality and a bed for the night in the home of Goldberry and Tom Bombadil after their perilous journey through The Old Forest.

The meeting closed with Robert asking everyone present if they wanted to go ahead. It would not be easy: we would be followed, there would be danger and we had to remember to protect ourselves at all times. Everyone said that they wished to take part in the Story.

Chapter 19

A Second Meeting

The next meeting was on 18 July and this time there were four more people present. We talked about the forthcoming eclipse of the sun on August 11 1999. An eclipse of the moon, as well as planetary alignments occur in January 2000. All these events signify the ending of an Age. The Sun and Moon and three planets, Uranus, Mars and Saturn, will form a grand cross in the sky. This is the last time this pattern at the time of a solar eclipse will be seen and it spells the end of the Era of The Cross of Suffering. Religion has killed more people than any other institution.

Tups who lives in Norfolk, told us of her experiences concerning the moon. One night as she took her dogs into the garden and stood waiting for them, she began to see a blue halo round the moon and then a beam of light coming down directly to her which followed her when she moved. In the continuing story of the Ring Tups takes the role of Galadriel and it is no coincidence that she lives in Norfolk, a flat country surrounded by water, which represents Galadriel's Mirror.

Judith, who takes the role of Pippin, had been looking at a bright star through binoculars. Sometimes it changed into a large snowflake and at other times a rainbow pyramid. Robert told us that the snowflake, of which there are no two alike, represents each individual soul. The rainbow pyramid symbolises many things: a focal point for energy to pass between the different levels, the marriage between heaven and earth, access to the stars. The star, of course, is the Silmaril that was cut from the very crown of the Dark Lord by the daring of Beren and Luthien and was eventually placed in the heavens as a symbol of the ending of an Age.[8] It is also the Star of Bethlehem, which also marked the ending of an Age.

The realignment of the planets has had an effect on the relationship of men and women. Men and women are the two opposing forces of the Chalice. In the middle is the balance where male and female come together and produce life.

Aragorn found the White Tree, a sapling of the line of Nimloth growing on Mount Mindolluin, and there is a connection here with the thorn tree on Wearyall Hill at Glastonbury, which comes into bloom at Christmas time. Robert told us that the enduring legend that Joseph of Aramathea visited Britain with Jesus and planted the white thorn tree on Wearyall Hill is true, as with so many legends. The mystic, artist and poet, William Blake, was right: those feet did 'walk on England's green and pleasant land'. The Gold Tree was destroyed, just as the Sacred King was destroyed. White and gold are spiritual colours and are perfectly balanced.

The room where we meet in the Wye Valley has pictures of Jesus and Princess Diana on the wall. Diana and Mother Theresa represented the feminine principle of the Age. Diana is the Goddess in her role of Mother, the 'Queen of Hearts'; Mother Theresa, in caring for the dying in the slums of Bombay, was the Goddess in her death aspect. The third aspect of the Goddess, the Maid, is also alive and with us today. Robert said that we can call on their energy.

At the morning coffee break Cassie mentioned to Robert that whenever she came to these meetings she developed a pain in her shoulder. He replied that this was because when Frodo arrived at Rivendell he had a wound. Of course he had! He had not long ago been stabbed in the shoulder by one of the Ringwraiths. "If I were you, I would ask Aragorn to take you a different way". So she did, and imagined the friends going south from *The Prancing Pony* with Aragorn as their guide, instead of northeast. The pain in her shoulder disappeared. Without tampering with the main patterns, we had changed the Story for the better, certainly from Frodo's point of view.

Chapter 20

The Fellowship is Formed

Robert asked Caroline to assign the various roles to people, which proved to be a delicate and difficult task. She had been canvassing people to see which roles they felt drawn to and were willing to accept. In an aside to Cassie some months ago, Robert had mentioned that Enid was Samwise. She was a Yorkshire woman with forthright views, which also brought to mind the 'Gaffer's' decided views on most subjects - the Gaffer being Samwise's father whom he was very fond of quoting. And just like Samwise, she was stubborn, loyal and easily moved to tears. However, when the suggestion was put to her by Robert, she turned it down. Cassie chose not to say anything as she did not want to bring any pressure to bear, which in retrospect she thinks may have been a mistake. A little bit of persuading can often work wonders!

There was another meeting on 15 August. Robert gave us all helpful insights into the Story. Galadriel, Celeborn and Elrond oversee the journey from afar and send advice and protection. We were to remember to use their energy. It is a story of losses and gains – the companions have to let Bill the pony loose, for example, to Samwise's great distress, because they cannot take a pony through the mines of Moria.

Boromir sets Frodo off on his path to Mordor. This takes place at the Falls of Rauros on the great river Anduin. Boromir is beginning to succumb to the evil vibrations of the One Ring and attempts to take the Ring off Frodo by force. Frodo understands that it is the evil power of the Ring that has turned the noble Boromir into this raving creature and it gives him the final courage to set off directly East towards Mordor with Samwise. We realised that seemingly disastrous events in the Quest have a beneficial outcome and are a necessary part of the help given the Nine on their journey. Aragorn's agony of indecision was solved for him at a stroke by the Fellowship being broken up in this seemingly disastrous manner - Frodo and Samwise are now beyond reach, Boromir is dead. He is now free, with the help of Legolas and Gimli, to pursue the orcs who have carried off Merry and Pippin. It was unsettling to be told that orcs would be represented in life as real people. Robert put Caroline in charge of the Nine just as Aragorn had been Gandalf's number two on the Quest.

In the end Cassie's choice of Samwise had fallen on Hilary but she was dismayed by Robert's reaction on hearing the news. He did not think it a good choice and said that Cassie would have to carry her instead of the other way round. Frodo would not have been able to complete the Quest without the support of Samwise who deprived himself of food and water to help sustain Frodo when he was in a very bad way. At the bitter end,

Samwise somehow found the strength to carry Frodo on his back up the slope of the volcano. Cassie could see the source of the problem, which was not an uncommon one. Hilary had told her that she found it hard to read *The Lord of the Rings* and even harder to remember the Story.

This was a problem for a number of people given roles in the Story. Fortunately, it would not hinder us anchoring the energies at various times even though we might not have picked up on the clues and therefore be unaware that we were temporarily re-enacting a scene from the original Story. Robert gave an example of just such a clue by mentioning that not far from here was a street called 'Underhill'. This was where Bilbo and then Frodo lived. It was also the false name given Frodo by Gandalf under which he was to travel as, to Frodo's horror, Gandalf had told him that the name of 'Baggins' was known to The Dark Lord. The name had been given to him by Gollum under torture.

In the event, Hilary was to opt out early on and to cease coming to the regular meetings that took place. Over the coming years we would often wonder who was taking the role of Samwise, as it was unclear. Only recently did we work out who, for a time, had taken on that role. Also, in February 2006, a chance remark from Robert gave us a further insight, which showed just how ingeniously the problem was solved.

Finally, the line-up was - the hobbits: Annesley – Merry, Judith – Pippin, Hilary – Samwise, Frodo – Cassie. The other members of the Nine were Naomi as Gimli the dwarf, Jenny – Celeborn, Karen – Boromir, Caroline – Aragorn and Robert as Gandalf. Julia was Elrond, Tups – Galadriel, Tess – Arwen, Craig – Eomer, Barbara – Eowyn, Enid – King Theoden and Clarissa as Beregond of the Royal Guard of Minas Tirith whose actions saved the life of Faramir. Jenny became Legolas after the original choice had dropped out – a character much better suited to her doughty personality! It was not necessary to hand out all the roles at this stage and Robert had said that people would dip in and out of the characters depending on which part of the story we were attracting by our actions. Only Cassie and Caroline would remain as Frodo and Aragorn throughout the quest. Unfortunately, one or two were dissatisfied with their roles and this meant that there was an underlying resentment in some quarters. As Robert was to say at a later date, "Too many people want to be King."

During the lunch break, we all went outside where we stood high on the hillside with its stunning views and large expanse of sky. Robert pointed to the sky asking us what we saw. To the amazement of all, a cloud could be seen forming into the shape of the Loch Ness monster with four rings looped on its arched neck. The monster rapidly changed into a horse, then a turtle, a whale and a duck. These were clues as to where we might find four Rings of Power. Strangely enough, at about this time in the 'Friends' sitcom, Joey and Chandler's pet duck swallows a gold ring. To us it seemed that the physical world was responding to the Story taking place at the etheric level because of the inescapable truth, 'As above, so below'.

At the end of the afternoon the weather had changed and become dark. Again, Robert took us outside saying that the battle lines had been drawn and told us to look at the sky. We could all see two long lines of cloud, a thicker white band above and a dark one directly below matching the dimensions of the band above, clearly showing us that the battle lines had been drawn. The Nine Walkers were leaving the safety of Rivendell and starting on their journey. We were instructed that each member of the Nine had the love of his land, devotion to his master and the desire to go home. Some would play out the scenes involving the characters they represent in the book and we would experience the difficulties and problems in real life.

Robert had pointed out that there were several working groups and he mentioned Tups and Jenny, Cassie and Caroline and himself and Hilary. We were to act as one but apart. These groups were to find Rings and not be corrupted by them. He also, confusingly at the time, said that Rings were 'proliferating' at the physical level. With hindsight we take this to mean the ever-increasing number of roundabouts throughout the country to tackle the increased volume of cars on the roads.

Time is fluid so some scenes would be repeated until the lesson was learnt. On at least three occasions over the next five years Robert was to mention at his talks that Cassie was back in Hobbiton at the very beginning of the Quest!   It reminded us of the game of Snakes and Ladders when you are at the top of the board and think you are nearly home but then land on the longest snake on the board and slither down to about three squares from the beginning. What was meant by 'lessons to be learnt', and what were the 'blunders' in humanity's history that we had to set right? We did not realise that we had to actually find out what they were so we would understand how to correct them, nor did we realise that we had to take into account the history of humanity <u>since</u> the time of the *Lord of the Rings* to the present day. For a long time we were doomed to go on repeating the mistakes and blunders because we did not know what they were!   Therefore, for many years we were not in a position to correct them. In effect, the story told in The Lord of the Rings is a continuing one just as Samwise and Frodo discovered. Of course we had not been left totally helpless as Robert's talks contained many of the clues we needed to recreate those lost chapters in our history.

How does the interaction between the dimensions work?   If our circumstances at the physical plane become perilous then we will attract a similar energy in the Story. Likewise, if circumstances are safe and happy we will find ourselves re-enacting such scenes as those of the celebrations immediately after the battle and fall of Sauron. We suspect it also worked the other way: the interacting energy could influence us to enter or create dangerous situations similar to those being repeated in the original story.

Cassie and Caroline had already seen this in action. Cassie had been influenced to leave Northampton and set up home in Salisbury by a feeling of restlessness and the fact that all avenues appeared closed in Northampton. Caroline was temporarily without a home and had entered upon a period of wandering from place to place. This reflected Aragorn's life at this stage of the story. Many years ago Elrond, his foster father, had revealed to him his royal lineage and the high doom laid upon him. If he were to fail, he and his race would disappear from Middle Earth. He therefore began a long and weary fifty year period of self-imposed exile in which he became the hardiest of all living men, travelling far and wide, even to the East, to learn the ways of the those people and of the Enemy. The desperate Quest to destroy the Ring was the culmination for Aragorn of all those years of preparation.

During the coming years we slowly came to understand that it was not just at one level we needed to get the story right, but on many levels. The story had become trapped on successive planes as the planet fell down the energy levels over many thousands of years.

Chapter 21

Two Wormtongues

As we were crossing the Severn Bridge on our return journey a magnificent rainbow appeared spanning the river from one end of the bridge to the other but something rather strange happened as we drove across. One end of the rainbow unmistakably kept pace with the rear of our vehicle and then finally merged with the other end and disappeared. We could find no explanation for this, so mentioned the phenomenon to Robert on the off chance that he might elucidate. The answer came that it was a sign that we were being protected by angels.

We always enjoy the return journey to Salisbury if the weather is good because the late afternoon atmosphere casts a golden glow over the countryside. It was one of those blue and white cloudy skies that draw the attention and we noticed something rather unusual in the shape of the clouds, which was quite unmistakable. It was a snake with the upper body raised and mouth wide open as if to strike. The head was disproportionately large as the body was disproportionately short. Then another, identical snake formed so that it was facing the other, also rearing up with a wide-open mouth. It was as if the two were about to fight. What did it mean? We were also very puzzled by their short bodies.

About two weeks later it suddenly came to us. One of them at least was Wormtongue. The short body was that of a worm and the open mouth suggested a snake's tongue. Gandalf refers to this traitor - chief advisor to King Theoden no less - as a snake, as he was in league with the enemy. Wormtongue had become Saruman's spy and his task, using lies and insinuation, was to undermine the King so he became confused and weak and mistrusted the very people who truly loved him.

However, we were still puzzled. Why were there two Wormtongues facing each other in such a combative fashion when in the original story there was only one? Much later, we understood they could also represent the two Kings of the solar year fighting for the love of the Queen. At one stage in the evolution of this Cult the two kings were made to fight to the death. Also, here is to be found the origins of that potent mix called The Love Triangle. As midsummer drew near, the King knew he was about to be supplanted in the Queen's affections by the 'twin' King and his terror and fury knew no bounds.

In the meantime, we remembered the behaviour of one of the people at the meeting we had just left who, we suddenly realised, was clearly taking the part of Wormtongue.

Chapter 22

Gollum

We continued to go to Robert's workshops, which were always fascinating. He would cover many topics and we realised after a time that one of the things he did, although it was not at all apparent, was to go round every individual in turn pinpointing a problematic area of their lives and suggesting various ways they might help themselves. It was done as a general address and was interesting and helpful for all.

At a workshop, held a few months after the meetings at Rivendell had ended, Robert was, unusually, giving a talk at Jean's house in Lydney. It was the lunch break when Cassie suddenly realised the person sitting next to her was taking the part of Gollum. There were unmistakable points of comparison to be drawn between the two. Both were unusually short – Gollum was related to hobbits or 'halflings' because they were half the size of a man - and both had large pale, green eyes. She was also Cassie's friend and it was through Cassie that she had begun coming to Robert's workshops. This is in keeping with the story as Gollum was drawn to Frodo by the power of the Ring. He also becomes Frodo's and Samwise's constant companion through the dangerous lands close to Sauron's realm as he had agreed to be their guide.[9]

We had met in November 1998 at a weekend course in the Malvern Hills. We both had two daughters of similar ages and had agreed to meet up after the course. She and her two daughters came for a visit to Salisbury and we went to their home for a weekend.

Gollum's story is a sad one. It was his misfortune to become the owner of the One Ring with a power far beyond his mind and body so he was quickly enslaved and his life became a living hell, bereft of friends, love and joy in the beauty of the physical world. Gollum also nursed a strong sense of rejection. This was because, having discovered that the One Ring made him invisible, he had taken to spying on people in his community and maliciously causing trouble. In the end, he was cast out by the matriarch of his family. Cassie's friend also lived with a sense of rejection by her family as she was put up for adoption.

The tragedy was that she began to stir up trouble and, so, experienced another rejection. She had many private consultations with Robert who showed infinite patience and, when she finally left the group, he told us all that she would eventually have to be brought back. And that we realised, was the key. One way of getting the story right would have been the rehabilitation of Gollum, and there had been a chance that we might have succeeded, as it had begun well.

She telephoned Cassie out of the blue after all the trouble but Cassie had mixed feelings. We had not been directly involved in all the problems as we had only attended a few of Robert's talks after the meetings at Rivendell ended and the Walkers had set out. Cassie's loyalties were being pulled in opposite directions as she still felt sympathy for this person. However, she had behaved badly towards Caroline/Aragorn.

Just like Aragorn with Gollum, Caroline had little sympathy and advised Cassie against seeing this person, particularly in view of the role she had taken on. For these reasons Cassie felt unable to open the door of friendship to her again, but experienced a lingering regret.

It was also she who had been disruptive during the meeting when Caroline was trying to help people chose their 'roles'. Normally quiet and seemingly moderate, it was as if she was possessed and had turned into quite a different person. It is obvious to us now that the energy of Gollum's antipathy for Caroline/Aragorn was manifesting during that meeting because Caroline was taking a leading role.[10] At the same time we can see that she was simultaneously playing the part of Wormtongue, as mentioned above, as her underhand methods were identical.

With the benefit of hindsight we realise that the only people who were aware of the part this person was actually taking were those who had had direct contact with Gollum in the original story. These were Gandalf/Robert, Aragorn/Caroline and Frodo/Cassie. Of course Samwise knew Gollum well but at this point we did not know who had taken the part.

Cassie also had an encounter with the real Gollum. At the very first talk given by Robert in Lydney, which we attended, she developed acute earache in her left ear which, thereafter, would re-occur only during Robert's workshops. When she asked him what might be causing these, he replied cryptically that someone was trying to get through to her but that she was resisting. She was puzzled as she was unaware she was resisting anything.

This went on for quite some time until finally one day, two years later, after a bout of earache, she sat down in a particularly determined frame of mind and asked for the person who was trying to get through to her to say what it was they wished to say, and waited. To her amazement, she suddenly heard a hissing voice in her ear, which she knew immediately to be Gollum's because it was exactly as she imagined it would sound. The voice simply hissed 'Where is it: where is the Ring?' She was so taken unawares that it was hard to collect her thoughts but she does remember telling him that she did not have the Ring, that it was invisible to her, that we were cleansing it regularly, and that we had just recently cleansed it. She suggested that he visit Robert whom she felt sure would be able to help him - Gandalf had felt compassion for Gollum and had believed in the possibility of his redemption. She waited but there was no response and after a little while she could tell that he had gone.

Chapter 23

A Ring at White Horse Hill

The day was 27 August (1999), and we were setting off on a sunny day to try and find one of the Rings of Power. It was relatively easy for us to jump into the car at a weekend and set off as Caroline had come to live with Cassie and daughters in May of that year. It was in keeping with the story that Strider/Aragorn should be with Frodo, as the hobbits would never have reached Rivendell (in August) without Strider as their guide.

Robert had given all of us a big clue as to the whereabouts of the Ring connected with a horse. He had previously mentioned that he wanted us to go to the chalk hill-figure of the White Horse at Uffington, with Dragon Hill nearby and Wayland's Smithy, a Neolithic long barrow, a mile and a half away along the Ridgeway. It seemed obvious that this was where we would find the first Ring.

Realising by now that the Universe would be giving us helpful hints, we kept a lookout as we drove along and the first sign was a corn-drying firm called "Gandalf".

On reaching the Vale of the White Horse we had our first view of this most graceful and ancient of the white horses believed to date back to the first century BC, or further, as it resembles the stylised horses on coins used by the Celtic Belgae tribe. We had our usual picnic with the whole of the Vale with its chequered, golden fields of late summer corn laid out before us and then made our way up the hill. All of a sudden the weather changed and white and dark clouds appeared over the horizon.

Our first walk round the outline of the horse, being careful to keep to the grass, proved fruitless so far as finding a ring was concerned. But what was significant was the sudden appearance of a youngish man dressed very conventionally in blue shirt and khaki chinos but, strangely for these days, he had a pipe stuck in the corner of his mouth, but no smoke was coming from it. He was like an actor who wishes to project a certain image but has got one of the props slightly wrong. He seemed to avoid our gaze. After a minute or so we turned round to have another look at him so that he would be aware that we knew who he was, to find him looking back at us. He turned hastily away and disappeared over the brow of the hill.

We continued to walk around looking for a clue which would suggest the point of power. We noticed a small flock of seagulls circling overhead. We hoped that one of them would come down and mark the exact spot but the flock flew away. Two more flocks appeared, circled for a while and then flew off, so at least we knew we were in the right general area. Members of the public had, meanwhile, been coming and going and we noticed a man with a black dog on whom we kept an eye. We were not having much luck, so Cassie thought she would walk over to nearby Dragon Hill. As we still had to walk a mile and a half to Wayland's Smithy and back and Caroline was feeling rather tired that day, she declined to accompany her. Cassie returned saying that it had a very unpleasant atmosphere.

After our experience at Fisherton Island where we found a physical Ring, we had again been looking for a physical object. It suddenly dawned on us that the Ring was at the etheric level and therefore invisible. All we need do was find the place of power and summon the Ring. We stood for a while just admiring the stunning view of vale and sky. Looking hopefully at the sky for a clue, one was given. The dense white clouds shifted to enclose a space of blue sky. The patch of blue grew smaller and smaller until it became rectangular in shape, resembling the head of the White Horse! We should have worked it out for ourselves, as we knew from the pagan cults that the head and the eye are seats of power. In the Cult of the Sacred King, one eye in particular was believed to be vested with great power so that a person needed to be shielded from that awesome power lest they be struck dead.[11]

Positioning ourselves near the eye we asked the Ring to come into Cassie's hand. She felt the familiar tingling in her palm, meaning the Ring had arrived, and put it safely away in her pocket wrapped in a handkerchief. As she did so, the sun came out from behind the clouds and shone down on both the hill of the White Horse and Dragon Hill, but the latter quickly became dark again. At the time we took this to mean that Dragon Hill needed clearing, but we were only partly right. This was not the only reason.

We now had to go to Wayland's Smithy along the ancient route on the top of the downs known as the

Ridgeway, taking in the Iron Age fort of Uffington Castle on our way. As we walked, we noticed that the sun, which had once again gone behind clouds, was sending out rays in an exact replica of ancient Egyptian pictures from the Eighteenth Dynasty: the rays from the sun, representing Aten, the One God introduced by the Pharaoh, Akhenaten. This magnificent panorama continued for the length of our walk to Wayland's Smithy, which was beautiful, bordered by hedges of hawthorn and sloe and the late-flowering wild flowers of the chalk downs such as scabious and harebell. We saw more butterflies, mostly fritillaries, than we had seen all summer. The views over the downs were stunning, peaceful and timeless. In the hedge a wren was twittering to itself as it hopped among the twigs looking for insects. However behind us, and gradually getting nearer - eventually, to about fifty yards - was a young man in an orange and green rugby shirt. We didn't think this suspicious until, having overtaking a couple and their two children, we looked back only to find that he was nowhere to be seen. There was no way he, realistically, could have disappeared. Yet another 'person' from the Other Side taking an interest in our activities. Later, Robert told us that this person had come in through a 'time porthole' and that we must return and close it down so that it could never be used again. This we did on another occasion not long after.

We had been walking for about forty minutes and were beginning to think we had taken a wrong turning, when we finally came across the mysterious ring of beech trees, which encloses the famous barrow. The trees were surrounded by a field of ripe wheat which was in the process of being harvested. In fact, as we circled the grove of beech trees, so did the combine harvester. There was a curious atmosphere. It was as if we had been transported back to the time when it was built, a time both primitive and innocent. We walked around the barrow in the late afternoon sunshine and said a silent prayer as a preliminary to clearing the site on our return home.

On our way home we had another reminder of the quest we were on and of the fact that everything was being repeated, all the strands of Earth's history coming together. In the evening sky was a long, thin grey cloud in the unmistakable shape of an enormous sword. In the centre there was even a dark line: it was Anduril, sword of Aragon, newly reforged from the shards of Narsil. Narsil was the sword of Elendil, leader of the faithful Numenoreans in their exile in Middle Earth after the destruction of the island of Numenor. The sword was broken in combat between Elendil and the Dark Lord, which ended the long, seven-year war. Elendil and Gil-galad both fell in battle but Isildur cut the finger with the Ring on it from Sauron's hand with the hilt-shard of his father's sword. As in *The Lord of the Rings*, Narsil has been reforged and given the name of Anduril, Flame of the West.

Returning to the house, we immediately put the Ring into the specially protected little Middle Eastern box in the second of the four compartments alongside the Ring we had found on Fisherton Island. As it was the weekend, we were not able to contact Robert until Monday evening and the first thing he said to us was that we had become careless and hadn't protected ourselves sufficiently. He always impressed upon us the need to protect ourselves. Luckily for us, he was still watching over us and rescuing us when we were foolish or neglectful. Had we, he asked, noticed the white clouds coming up behind us as we made our way from the car park to White Horse Hill? Those clouds had fired many black darts into us and he had spent a very long time painstakingly removing them. What might have happened had they not been removed? Doubtless, we would have fallen sick in some way and continued indefinitely in low health.

We had also brought something nasty back with us and hadn't we noticed a change in the weather and how cold our sitting room had become? Looking back we did remember thinking that the week-end in our part of the world had not been as good as forecast and feeling irritated that the sitting room was so cold and uninviting. But we had neglected to put two and two together. We immediately cleared the house and felt a great deal warmer.

We never asked, and Robert never volunteered, precisely what had attached itself to us. Nor did we ask who fired the black darts. Perhaps it was best for us not to know so that our minds would not dwell on the image and give it power. In his talks Robert has said that evil exists only in the minds of man and Shakespeare said the same thing: 'There is nothing good nor bad but thinking makes it so.' Ever in our minds were Robert's words that the less information he gave us, the less his opposite number was able to advise <u>his</u> helpers. In the best-selling series of books by David Eddings, which begin with *The Mallorean*, the set-up is identical. The reason that the task is taken up by weaker humans and hobbits is to limit the awesome power that the major protagonists might unleash should there be a direct confrontation between such as, say, The Dark Lord and Gandalf. In Tolkien's story, the Dark Lord's chief lieutenant - leader of the Black Riders - and Gandalf, come close to such a confrontation at the ruined gates of the City of Gondor but, at the very moment of testing, they are miraculously spared by the dawn crowing of the cock and the simultaneous blowing of a multitude of horns announcing the arrival of the Riders of The Mark, who have come to the aid of Gondor.

Chapter 24

A Ring at Dragon Hill

Robert did, however, confirm that we had the Ring, but he told us that we had to return to Dragon Hill. We were rather perplexed by this enigmatic statement, but it was obviously something to do with the dragon. We had already come to the conclusion that the White Horse was, in fact, a dragon. Not least because of its forked tongue, quite apart from the fact that its long thin body and excessively long tail is quite unhorse-like. Strangely, the forked tongue is never mentioned in any of the several books we have read on the subject.

It was then that the image came to Cassie that the shape of the hill was like the vast mound of jewels, gold, armour and other precious things that dragons were wont to sleep on after their avaricious labours. She also remembered reading how the foundation of each of the dwarves' hoards of treasure was a Ring - seven of the Rings of Power had been given to the dwarf kings. The effect of a Ring of Power on a dwarf was different to that of men, who faded to become Ringwraiths, completely in Sauron's power. It intensified the dwarves' lust for gold. These treasure hoards had later been plundered by dragons, so Cassie realised that it was feasible that there was a *second* Ring, which was over Dragon Hill. The shape of the hill could even be said to resemble a great pile of treasure topped with a sleeping dragon just like Tolkien's Smaug in his book *The Hobbit.* She dowsed and found that, indeed, there was another ring at Dragon Hill at the etheric level, which was exerting an evil influence on the surrounding area.

Two days' later, on 29 August, we set off again, and this time we had protected ourselves properly. As we approached the White Horse we observed a girl with a black Labrador talking into a mobile telephone who looked up as we approached. Caroline made a note to keep an eye on her. We walked down to the Horse and noticed something else strange about it: the two, so-called, ears are of quite a different shape and arranged at some distance apart. One 'ear' is a thin, oblong protrusion and the other, at the very top of the head, is much larger and conical in shape - in fact, it is like a spike or a short horn. Viewed with no preconceived ideas, it is quite unfeasible as an ear. There is also a second spike on one of the front legs. We were to learn later that we were half right about it being a dragon, but there was a further insight into its full significance.

We proceeded to walk down the slope over to Dragon Hill. There were one or two people around but Caroline managed to get the Ring into her hand, again at the etheric level, and put it straight into her pocket with no trouble. As we reached the brow of the hill, we noticed that the first girl with the Labrador had disappeared to be replaced by another, older woman with yet another black dog, a very large, odd-looking poodle. It was a dog in all respects except for its eyes, which, sinisterly, were very un-dog like. In fact, they were human with a bright, knowing, aggressive stare. And stare it did. The woman, on the other hand, had her face turned away. After we had passed them Caroline turned to try and catch her eye, only to find her staring at us. Once again, as with the youngish man we had encountered on our previous visit, she turned hastily away. Later, she asked Robert why these manifestations from the Other Side seemed to be avoiding our gaze and he replied that they were frightened of us, which was good news so far as we were concerned.

We made our way back down the hill to the car park and, as we did so, we glanced up at the sky and there was the longest strip of cloud we had ever seen. It stretched from one horizon to the other like a gigantic spine. Then one of us noticed that there were distinct vertebrae, as distinct as if it were a photograph. In fact it was exactly like the spine of the dinosaur skeleton at the Natural History Museum in London, the end even thinning away like a tail. For 'dinosaur' read 'dragon' which had obviously been transported to the Great Treasure in the Sky. It reminded us of the description given of Smaug's bare bones lying at the bottom of the Lake. There he had plummeted to his ruin after being shot by The Black Arrow in the pale yellow hollow over his heart which was the only vulnerable place in his gem encrusted belly.[12]

After driving on a little way, we noticed that the cloud was still there but now it looked fatter like a rib cage, and there appeared to be a sword laid across. At that we stopped the car and got out to have a better look. There was indeed a cloud that looked exactly like a broadsword cutting into the underbelly of the rib cage. Cassie, who had just been reading Tolkien's *The Silmarillion*, then realised that the second dragon must be Glaurung who appears in that book. Glaurung was killed by Turin Turambar from beneath, just as the sword was showing us. The dragon had flung its body across the chasm of a deep ravine and Turin had climbed the cliff directly underneath and thrust the Blacksword, Gurthang, up to the hilt into the dragon's soft underbelly. It is curious that the weapons which killed the two dragons were both renowned and called 'Black'. Is it an example of history repeating itself during the great sweep of time covered in Tolkien's chronicles of Middle Earth? A further example springs to mind. Both the Silmaril, which was recovered by Beren and Luthien, and the Arkenstone, were large gems beyond price: both were used as bargaining counters.[13]

It seemed that by removing the evil Rings of Power both dragons had lost their grip at the lower astral so enabling their deaths in the story to be re-enacted. Our conscious acknowledgment of this pinned the story down at the dense physical thus clearing it from a parallel dimension.

As usual, we reported back to Robert. We told him that we thought the White Horse was really a dragon, and mentioned the forked tongue and the two spikes. He replied that although it was a dragon now, at a time in the past it had been a unicorn - that perfect symbol of purity, hence the spike, which had originally been a horn. In later times when the Earth's vibrations had become ever lower, it had been taken over by the dark forces as represented by the dragon, Glaurung, and the unicorn had gradually been altered to look more like a dragon. In fact, there is definite evidence at the site that the 'horse' was at one time a great deal fatter.

Just a week after our second visit there was a programme on television with the title *Steve Irwin's Deadly Dragons*. The dragons in question are the Komono dragons of Indonesia, the biggest and most dangerous lizards alive today and remarkably like the dragon of myth and legend. In a scene in the programme, as several of these creatures tear at the carcass of a deer, one only needed to magnify their size to get a picture of what dragons must have looked like when they ruled the earth, as they did at the dawn of Earth's history. There is no enduring myth that is not based on a true story.

And just as we finished going over these chapters on the deaths of the two dragons, we experience further synchronicities. On the very day, our copy of *The Week* (27 January 2007) arrived through the post and on the cover was a picture of an enormous, fiery, orange and yellow dragon in space (i.e. at another dimension) fiercely breathing destructive fire over a satellite. China had just successfully tested an anti-satellite missile on one of its own weather satellites. Less than a week later there was wide media coverage of David Beckham agreeing to play the role of St George in the ancient legend of St George slaying the Dragon. And one final touch: Cassie had dinner with friends on Saturday 27 January and noticed in their room a large, serpentine dragon woven in an orange and green coloured straw, which they had brought back from Thailand.

Chapter 25

The Opposition

After the last meeting at Rivendell on 15 August Robert had told us that the battle lines were now drawn. He also warned us that, as Frodo and Aragorn, we would be particularly targeted by the Forces of the Left and that we should be on our guard.

Almost immediately, on returning to Salisbury, Caroline had a curious incident. She and a friend were having an evening drink in the garden of a hotel when she became aware of a fat, squat man who had sat down fairly near her with a huge cigar in one hand and a tankard of beer in the other. She became aware of him as there was a sinister stillness about him as if he were listening to the conversation they were having, which, rather stupidly, was to do with Cassie's and her clearing work and, once again, the prop of the huge cigar looked old-fashioned and phoney. She challenged him in her mind and a minute later, to her great satisfaction, saw him jump to his feet, as if he had been stung by a bee, and lumber off as fast as he was able. However, she was puzzled when, after a few minutes, he returned, but by then she and her friend were ready to leave. Stupidly as it turned out, she looked at him as they walked away and he looked back, unlike the first one who had avoided her gaze.

When she mentioned this incident to Robert he said that the man who returned was not the same entity as the first man. He said the Other Side would send 'people' like that until there was one who was stronger than she and had she noticed a twinge of pain when he had looked at her? And indeed she had. She had felt a twinge of pain in her hip, which at the time, was a weak point. We now know that we should not challenge anyone by looking at them, only in our minds.

On several subsequent occasions, we met extremely unpleasant people in the city. They were often women invariably dressed in out-of-fashion black clothes and exuding an air of menace. We would meet them in some place, usually a shop, and then, as we left the shop, eerily, we would see them again coming in the opposite direction.

On one horrible occasion, Caroline was in an aisle in a supermarket when it suddenly emptied and she was left alone while a frighteningly tall woman, dressed all in black and walking with a stick (they were also often disabled in some way), advanced on her and stood behind her exuding menace as she dithered over a purchase with every hair on her head prickling. She asked Robert what was the point of this, and he said that she was being tested.

Chapter 26

Tom Bombadil and Crows

Around this time, late summer, we interfaced with the part of the story where the hobbits are twice rescued by Tom Bombadil. It is at an early stage in the story before the hobbits reach the sanctuary of Rivendell. The Hobbits are being pursued by the Black Riders in their own country, The Shire, and are forced to take the decision to go through the Old Forest with its hostile reputation, as the only way of shaking off the pursuit. There, they fall into the deadly grip of Old Man Willow but are rescued in the nick of time by Tom Bombadil who takes them to his home where he lives with the lovely Goldberry. Robert told us that we would be visiting an orchard by a river, and to be aware of the presence of Tom Bombadil and Goldberry.

We had, in fact, already planned to go for a walk that day in the Woodford Valley alongside a river where there is an orchard and, before setting off, we called in at the pub, as we were both thirsty. There was no one else there and we were in no doubt that the publican and his wife, a lovely young girl with golden hair, were Tom and Goldberry. We duly walked past an orchard which ran down to the river and, after that, we felt that we were being accompanied. We even passed an ancient willow with a huge crack in its trunk like Old Man

Willow. We stopped to look at some horses in a field who threw up their heads and stared and stared at us as if they couldn't believe what they were seeing. It was only when we eventually walked on that they returned to their grazing. Had they seen Tom and Goldberry?

Not long after this we both experienced incidents which echoed those of the first leg of the Quest shortly after the Fellowship had set out from Rivendell. The first for Caroline was the loud cawing of a crow as she left the house. It was so insistent that she looked around to see where it was coming from and eventually noticed a single crow on top of a chimney. As soon as it saw her it flew off as if on a mission. She felt a definite unease. Then as she walked along she passed a tree full of rooks who, at her approach, flew off making a great din. Cassie also had one or two experiences involving crows. The crows, of course, were the crebains, that were flying over Hollin and spying out the land between the Mountains and the River Greyflood and which Aragorn saw as he kept watch. Aragorn knew they had come from way south, close to where Saruman dwelt. Little did he realise that it was indeed Saruman, turned traitor, who had sent the crows in the hope of intercepting the Ring and taking it for himself. The Nine Walkers now had to go without fire and travel only by night.

The next incident was on a walk when Caroline came across a young man with two Dobermans. On noticing her they raced towards her and their owner called them, as if they were out of control. Feigning complete absence of fear, which was far from the way she really felt, she held her ground and the young man eventually caught up with them and managed to put on their leads. The dogs represented the terrifying, but illusionary, wargs/wolves the company battled with one night shortly after the spying flocks of crows.

Chapter 27

An Owl in a Blossom Tree

Around this time Caroline had two dreams. She was standing by a tree with white blossom in which perched a Little Owl, a bird sacred to the Goddess, in particular, the Greek Goddess of Wisdom, Athena. A man and a woman came along and took the owl away with them. Much dismayed, she ran after them and said, 'You are not supposed to take the owl away from the tree', and managed to persuade them to return with her and place it back in the branches. When she told Robert about this dream he replied, 'So you left the Tree?' At first she was puzzled by this remark.

Later, she interpreted the dream thus: the tree is the White Tree, Nimloth (later renamed Telperion), whose seed Isildur brought with him over the waters to Middle Earth and which grew in the courts of the Kings. It was the symbol of the Royal Line of Luthien and there was a prophecy of long ago saying the Line of Luthien would never die. The Royal Line, therefore, passes through the female line, just as it did in Egyptian times and also in France. The owl, symbol of the Goddess, is Arwen who, by her marriage to Aragorn, ensured the continuance of the Royal Line through the ages of humankind. This was why Caroline/Aragorn was so concerned at the owl being removed from the tree.

It was the task of Aragorn, Isildur's heir, to keep hope, as symbolised by the White Tree, alive. By leaving it, Caroline had left it unguarded. In other words, she was placed in an impossible Catch 22 situation. If she stayed by the tree, the owl was abducted: if she went after the owl, the tree was left unprotected. It therefore reflects Aragorn's difficult position when the Nine Walkers have to decide what to do next on the journey, as The Ring, borne by Frodo, has to turn east towards Mordor. Aragorn must decide whether to go west with Boromir to Minas Tirith, which he yearns to do, or to go East with Frodo, whom he has sworn solemnly to help in his task of destroying the One Ring.

Yet another interpretation is that the Queen/Goddess has been removed from her rightful place. The reason for this is that she forfeited her position when the Queen, the Goddess's representative on Earth, became the cruel, bloodthirsty creature of the pagan cults. She was overthrown and it was then that she was taken away from the tree. Now is the time for the Queen/Goddess to be cleansed of that cruel image, which lives on in our subconscious minds, so that the owl can be restored to the White Tree. One of Aragorn's aims is to restore the Kingship of Men and he knows he cannot do this without a Queen by his side, hence Caroline/Aragorn going after the couple and telling them they cannot take the owl away from the Tree.

A dream may have several interpretations, as do Egyptian hieroglyphs – at the mundane, the symbolic and the esoteric (or hidden) levels.

We have just had another astonishing synchronicity. The very day - Monday 22 January 2007 - we edited this chapter a large A4 size, glossy pamphlet dropped through the letterbox from one of the local estate agents. On the front page was a close-up picture of a barn owl, with its heart-shaped white face, sitting in a pine tree, with one word written in large capital letters across the page – 'WISDOM'.

The second dream, as so often, was expressed in terms of the news of the day. A certain well-known person, who was in prison at the time, gave into Caroline's safekeeping a large diamond until he should leave prison and be able to give it to the woman he loved as an engagement ring for their forthcoming marriage. It was a particularly magnificent stone and brought to mind Galadriel's ring, Nenya, which was of adamantine and one of the three Elven Rings.[14] A few weeks' later, a friend showed her a beautiful crystal, very like a large diamond. Just before leaving, he handed it to her, saying, 'I feel I should give this to you.' The following day she was choosing a bottle of wine and her eye fell on an Australian red, which she was astonished to see came from a vineyard called Nanya. It seemed that we were in Lothlorien and Galadriel's Ring, for a while at least, was protecting us, the Nine Walkers, from the harsh world outside.

137

Chapter 28

Giant Spiders

In the summer, after Caroline had moved in with Cassie, she had a nasty encounter with a spider. She had just retired to bed when she suddenly noticed a truly enormous spider on the wall. Having thought she had conquered her arachnophobia, she suddenly realised that, at this size, she hadn't! Cassie and her daughter kindly offered to remove it and she went calmly to bed believing that it had been caught and thrown out of the house and garden. It was only the following day when she questioned her granddaughter that she learnt that the spider had actually fallen off the wall and scuttled away into a fireplace where they had been unable to catch it. They hadn't liked to tell her, as they knew she had to sleep in the room anyway. She therefore had to continue sleeping there in the knowledge that it was somewhere around.

It next turned up on its way to Cassie's bedroom. This time it was caught and thrown over the garden wall, only to be found back in the house a few days' later. This was obviously no ordinary spider. In other words, it was Shelob, the primordial and deeply evil giant spider who nearly does for Frodo and Sam as they make their way through the tunnel where she lurked at the top of the mountain pass in the land of the Dark Lord. It became obvious, therefore, that no amount of throwing out, or even killing it, would have had any effect. The only way to keep it away was to better protect the house at the spiritual level, which we were already doing, by mentally stopping up all drainpipes, chimneys, etc. This we did and Shelob, after once more being thrown over the garden wall, ceased her creepy scuttling.

A couple of months before this Caroline had visited the Serpentine Gallery in London and literally walked under Louise Bourgeois's enormous, steel spider before she realised what she was doing – in fact, something very strange for someone who disliked spiders. At the new Tate Modern art gallery at Bankside, which opened in May, there was an even bigger spider filling some of the space in the great former turbine hall. Finally, at the same time, two truly horrific sculptures of huge black spiders came to Salisbury's Cathedral Close for the May/June Art Festival held every year. Obviously, Shelob still lives.

And, as with so many towns and cities as discussed earlier, the 'ring' road around Salisbury, and roads leading off, resemble the body and legs of a spider. On this 'ring' road are placed further 'rings' in the form of roundabouts – five in total.

As we revised the above Caroline suddenly realised that, to have had so many experiences of enormous spiders, she must at this stage in the Story have been in the role of Samwise who engages in mortal battle with Shelob to save his beloved Master, Frodo. Then the reason she had walked beneath the sculpture of the spider in the Serpentine Gallery became clear: Samwise had finally managed to overcome Shelob by springing beneath her and, as she sank down upon him to crush him, he grasps his elven sword holding it point upwards and she impales herself upon the blade.

In real life, Caroline had also been earthing Samwise's supportive energy for Frodo. When staying with Cassie (Frodo) and her daughters, she gave support in various ways and continued to do so after moving out of the house in May.

Chapter 29

A Ring, a Tortoise and a Maze

In early September just after the school term had begun, we were given a clue as to the whereabouts of the Ring of Power connected with a turtle. One of Cassie's children had been clearing out some of her early childhood books, one of which was a children's version of *Aesop's Fables*. She passed it to Cassie, who happened to glance at the fable of the Hare and the Tortoise. It showed the race taking place round a spiral maze. As she gazed at the tortoise she realised that it was also a turtle and that the Ring was to be found in a maze: Robert confirmed this.

We now had to locate the maze. After some thought it seemed to us that the most likely one was the famous maze at Hampton Court. We suspected that the site of the palace was a former, ancient place of power and it is to such places of energy that the Rings of Power are attracted. Dowsing confirmed this.

We set off about midday so that we could have a picnic lunch en route and break the journey. We were quite surprised at the number of cars at the service station where we stopped but realised the reason soon after we set off again. It was people returning from holiday. The traffic had slowed down to anything between twenty miles an hour and a halt. We also thought that it might be phantom road works, real road works or an accident. As it transpired two hours, two accidents and twenty miles later, it was phantom road works *and* accidents. At one stage Cassie, who was driving, quite understandably wanted to get off at the next junction and return home, which was doubtless exactly what the Other Side hoped would happen. However, Caroline managed to persuade her that, as we had already been crawling for more than an hour, we might as well stick it out. Caroline regaled her with some of the funnier articles from one of the Sunday papers and finally, at the junction with the M25, the traffic started to flow again and we arrived at Hampton Court three and a half hours after we had set off from Salisbury.

The gardens were looking magnificent. Surrounded by late blooming summer flowers, we made our way towards the maze, keeping a lookout for anything untoward. As is always the case, the maze seemed very much smaller than when Caroline had last visited it as a young girl. We set off to try and find the centre. After the usual false hopes, and then remembering Winnie the Pooh's advice to Rabbit that if you go in the opposite direction to where you really want to end up, you have a very good chance of getting there, we finally found ourselves in the middle. Quickly asking that no one else should arrive, we stood between the two chestnut trees and Cassie commanded the Ring to come into her hand. She just had time to feel it and put it away in her pocket before several people joined us. She said afterwards that, unlike last time at the White Horse, the whole of her hand tingled and she saw in her mind's eye a particularly large and heavy Ring surrounded by gold light.

With a false sense of having accomplished our task we turned round, only to find that it was a great deal more difficult to get out than it had been to reach the middle. The maze was full of people cheerily going round and round giving advice to others on which paths not to take. We met a party of German students several of whom, as we passed them said, 'I am a potato' as if it was the greatest joke in the world. The whole expedition was beginning to take on a surreal air. Seeing a little girl in a bright orange fleece who seemed, and in fact, *was* lost, we adopted her and, feeling rather like the Mad Hatter, the March Hare and Alice, we all proceeded to be lost together. Finally, on seeing a gate with a sign saying "Emergency Exit", Caroline suddenly felt like getting out and called to the ticket girl to come and rescue us. Smiling a little, she came up with a key and we escaped with a feeling of relief. The girl we had adopted declined to come with us as she had just located her real family through a hole in the hedge.

Strolling down to some willows by a canal, we wondered if we were re-enacting the hobbits' experience in the Old Forest when they met Old Man Willow, the most ancient and malevolent tree in the Forest. The branches of the trees whipped around rather more than was warranted by the slight breeze and we thought the atmosphere seemed charged and slightly sinister. Feeling a heaviness in the air, we were glad to get away and walk towards the Teahouse for tea and scones before setting off for home. On the way back we were treated to the most spectacular sunset. The sky was pure, liquid gold.

We reported back to Robert who, when Caroline told him, slightly frivolously, how we had cheated and left the maze through the emergency exit, said, 'So you escaped.' Only then did we realise that the Other Side must have been preventing us from leaving. He said that this Ring was different from the others as it belonged to one of the Ringwraiths, or Nazguls (also known as the Black Riders), which is why it felt so heavy, and that we should put it in a different box. It had to be kept separately. Luckily Cassie, who collects little boxes, had one just the right size, with a wavy pattern picked out in brass on the lid, where we carefully deposited it. We put another amethyst crystal on top and spread its energy all the way round the box so it could not escape.

Doubtless, the opposition to collecting a Ring belonging to one of the Nazgul was stronger than usual and would go some way towards explaining the traffic hold-ups we experienced en route.

Chapter 30

Rings at Avebury

A large group of us encounter dragons, fairies and giants at the etheric level. This might be difficult for some to take on board but stories about these beings have come down to us in myth and legend through the ages and many people believe that such enduring tales are based on truth.

Annesley, a member of The Fellowship of the Nine who plays the role of Merry, came up with the idea that there was a ring at the Avebury stone circle in Wiltshire. Robert had told us that there were many rings which could be used by the Forces of the Left and that the group should collect as many as possible. She checked with Robert who confirmed that, indeed, there was a ring at Avebury, that it belonged to a Magus or Magician/Wizard, and it was still being used. After a little thought he said he had never been to Avebury and would like to go. He agreed therefore that it might be a good idea for some of the group, including the Nine Walkers, to meet there and would she arrange it? This she did and twelve of us plus Robert were due to meet up at Avebury on Tuesday, 5th October. In the event there turned out to be several rings.

It was a still, clear day with the promise of sunshine as we drove directly north. On meeting up with some of the others on our arrival we learnt that Robert would not be coming as two members of his family had 'flu' and he had to care for them. We were disappointed and were just wondering how to arrange our activities when, to our great relief, Robert turned up after all. He explained that his deception was necessary due to the forces ranged against him. He talked about the Michael and Mary lines which briefly merged within the stone circle and said that we needed to look for three of the Elven rings, one with a diamond, which had been hidden, never coming into the possession of Sauron. He proceeded to divide us into groups with himself, as it were, as Ringmaster, allocating a compass direction for each group to work from. Cassie and I were teamed up with Jean, (or Bilbo Baggins), who is a sensitive and would know when we were in danger and be able to warn and help to protect us.

Guided by Robert, we set off to collect three of the rings. As we approached the outer ditch and bank Robert asked Caroline what help she would call on and, as she was thinking about this, he prompted her to remember Cassie's and her experiences with Tom Bombadil and Goldberry, which we talk about later. Feeling happy and protected with these unseen companions, we clambered over the outer ditch to the north, turned westward and came to a grassy area surrounded by trees like a natural cathedral. We noticed a lot of feathers on the ground and followed the trail which led away until we came to a spot which we felt was the right place in a small grassy area enclosed by trees. Jean chose to stand a little way off while we called on the ring to materialise at the etheric level. We repeated this at two further sites. Jean, meanwhile, was very much aware of an oppressive atmosphere. Fairies had been guarding these rings and they were not at all happy at our taking them. She could feel anger being directed towards us. To propitiate them she left some small crystals, which she had with her, in the area and the atmosphere lightened.

Meanwhile, Annesley, Rex and Clarissa, had been given a south-westerly direction and were joined by Mary, Barbara and Enid. They went to the field near the Great Barn Museum where there is a line of Sarsen stones. Annesley collected an Elven ring near one of the stones which she put into a box she had brought with her. Robert said that we needed to know the exact position of the planets throughout the day, and that a particular stone formed part of a yod. This is an astrological term whereby two planets in sextile aspect to one another are both inconjunct to a third forming a "finger of fate" in the shape of a long, narrow triangle. Rex felt the different vibrations in one of the standing stones. He cleared and realigned energy lines at a subterranean level by finding bands on the stone. These energy lines go around the world. He moved on to stone no. 2 and Robert asked the group what they could pick up. They all felt a coldness round their legs and feet. Spirits of giants were present at this stone. The giants were old gods, and the group needed to ask for their permission to work at that place and use their energy. Bardic rituals had taken place there and beings were trapped in the stone. The souls were released and the area cleared. There were also white and black dragons at the site. At stone no. 3 Rex again realigned the energy lines. At stone no. 4 Robert said fairies were trapped in the stone and wanted to escape. The group released them and they indicated that the whole area round the stone needed clearing as, again, there were trapped souls. Judith, Karen and Jenny, the three other members of the group, had also spent the morning collecting rings, one belonging to a Magus.

We all met up again near a courtyard opposite the Great Barn Museum. Robert invited us to cross the threshold of the courtyard but no one accepted, as the atmosphere was horribly cold and forbidding. He then reminded us of what happened in *The Lord of the Rings* when the Nine Walkers arrived at the closed entrance to the Mines of Moria and the cryptic message above the great door, written in an ancient elven-tongue, was finally deciphered by Gandalf as, 'Speak, "Friend", and enter'. This we did and it was then safe for us to cross. Robert told us that this was the chapel where Gawain, one of the Knights of the Round Table, had gone to meet the headless Green Knight whose challenge he had accepted a year ago. He asked Cassie to tell us the story (See Appendix I). It was a place where many Sacred Kings had been sacrificed, and we joined hands and called on the Light to release them. Jean said that one of the kings had come and stood behind her and thanked us.

Walking to the road by the church where there were some cottages, Robert told us that bubonic plague had claimed many lives there and caused much suffering. We brought Light to the area. A black dragon had made its lair nearby and left a nasty cesspit, part of which was a place of black water. Part of the cesspool had been where the road now runs and as we walked along we felt physically ill at the precise spot. We purified the water and Robert told us to look at the sky where we just managed to catch a cloud in the process of changing quickly from the shape of a dragon to that of a lion. It was showing us that the trapped masculine energy of the sacrificed kings had been released and the rule of the king reinstated: the dominion of the dragon was at an end at last, at least at one level. So history does repeat itself. In Tokien's *The Hobbit* the death of the dragon, Smaug, paves the way for the restoration of the King of Dale.

We walked on back through the village in full sunshine, passing and clearing on the way several dragon lines, which caused a marked coldness round our feet.

Reaching the village pub we decided it was time for lunch and a break. It was a perfect autumn day, something we have come to expect when on an expedition out of doors with Robert, and we were able to eat outside. As we did so Jean, Cassie and Caroline noticed a threatening bank of black cloud advancing on us from the northeast. Calling on the forces of Light to help us we exerted our power to keep the dark forces at bay. The advance halted and the clouds began to recede. After lunch the whole group crossed the road into a field of standing stones and as we came abreast of the first stone Jean had a strong feeling of "protection", i.e. the outer ring was used for the protection of those within the circle. We moved towards the centre of the circle, which was opposite a small chapel, where Jean could hear children wailing and crying. Robert told us that this was a spot of great negativity where children had been sacrificed. She could feel great sorrow. We made a circle and joined hands, which we raised, and sent unconditional love to the children and prayed for them to be released. Immediately the energy started to build and Jean could see what looked like a huge diamond beginning to bury itself point first into the ground with small, sharp shafts of light flying off the surface of the diamond and away. The vision faded and we withdrew. Within the space of ten minutes Jean could hear children's laughter and the singing of nursery rhymes and knew that all was well. Afterwards, Robert told us that a Nazgul, one of the Ringwraiths, had been present.

We again split up, Annesley, Clarissa and Rex staying in the area to work with the stones and realign the energies while seven of us, directed by Robert, made our way to the outer bank to the north east to collect another ring. Robert told us to put forth all our power and, as we walked across the field towards the bank, we could see small, black clouds rising from a wood some distance away on a hill. Robert said witches were arraigned against us there and the clouds certainly appeared as serried ranks of a foe in battle formation. He then left us and returned to the others. Jean began to feel a very oppressive atmosphere and knew that there was another ring nearby. We reached the top of the bank and found the spot where the ring was to be collected. Jean felt very strongly that protection was paramount at this point, and arranged the rest of the group in a semi-circle around us. She told us that we should call strongly for the ring and she then turned away and faced a nearby wood at the bottom of the hill from where a great deal of negative energy was flowing. She asked for her light to be used as a wall to keep the negativity at bay. She called out to us that there were three rings to be collected. A strong and very cold wind began to blow until we had the rings safely in our keeping.

Robert had told us that when we had finished we should send Light down the energy line which stretched from Avebury, through Wayland's Smithy to the Wash in Norfolk and this we did, sending a golden ball of light spinning down the line to the sea. We had just started to walk away when Judith and Karen called to us to return. They told us that they had noticed a black cloud, which had suddenly built up and Judith, who is a sensitive, had received a message from the Magus. The rings had been under his protection and he was not at all pleased that we were taking them away. Judith said that we did not intend to use them and that we would take great care of them. He replied that we would have to swear an oath that we would protect them with our lives if needs be. This we did and he seemed satisfied that the rings were in safekeeping. The black cloud dispersed and the sun shone again. When we met up with the others, they too swore the oath.

We repaired once again to the pub for tea, where the twelve of us gathered round Robert at a long table above which there were three lights in the form of rings, one bigger than the rest. Robert said it had been a good day's work. He talked of certain matters pertaining to the group and then went on to speak of the yod, or finger of fate, which pointed to the south east towards Portsmouth. He reminded us that, in the past, England had been attacked along this coast line but now help was coming from the same quarter, just as Aragorn had sailed with a large force from the south coast of Middle Earth up the Anduin to the rescue of Minas Tirith, the same river up which in former times had come the enemy, the Corsairs of Umbar. Annesley then counted the rings and there were twelve altogether. Robert said that one of the rings that Cassie, Jean and Caroline had found in the morning was a Nazgul's, and had to be kept separately from the others. He designated a place of safekeeping for them. We then learnt that Rex had merged the Michael and Mary Line along its whole length, thus bringing together the Masculine and Feminine Principles. We only hope that those dowsing the Line in the future will not conclude that it is their dowsing that is at fault when they can only find one line!

Later, Robert told us that there had been five Ringwraiths at Avebury. He also mentioned that a powerful foe, whom he would have had to confront physically, had been prevented from reaching Avebury that day. Was this narrow escape to be compared with the moment in the story, where Gandalf, sitting on his white horse at the ruined gates of the White City, bars entrance to the Lord of the Nazgul?[15] As previously mentioned, Gandalf is spared by the timely intervention of the crowing of the cock and the arrival of their allies, the Men of Rohan. This was the Battle of the Pellennor Fields between Sauron's forces and those of the free West which, once again, was being played out at Avebury that day.

Robert, as he has told us, has an empty mind and can therefore be entirely in the present moment. And this is the way he works – he deals with what he comes across at that moment, which explains the odd and varied assortment of tasks we encountered that day in Avebury, from dragons to sacrificed children. That was what was there, so that was what we tackled.

´

Chapter 31

The Last Meeting of the Year

Five days' later the whole group, together with nine further members, were foregathered once again in the Wye Valley. Mary and Caroline had done some work on the astrological implications of our day at Avebury and today's meeting. Mary had software with which she could plot the exact position of the ascendant and planets throughout the day, and she brought along charts for each hour starting at dawn. We all studied them and Robert, Mary and Caroline discussed some of the implications. Robert said that the charts in time sequence matched what people did at Avebury that day. For instance, Rex realigning the magnetic lines of the Earth matched with certain changes on the charts. He had sent spiralled loops of energy, which Robert told us was the shape of infinity, in eight directions round the earth. Caroline described a yod, the finger of destiny or fate, with Venus and Mercury, messenger of the Gods, pointing to the end of the sign of Pisces in the period before noon on 5th October. Robert asked if this was a point of change and, more from intuition than reason, Caroline suggested that it signalled the ending of the Piscean Age, and Robert concurred with this. To all those who believe that the Piscean Age ended on a different date, that too is right. Pisces is a slippery customer and likes to disguise its true intentions. The charts for Sunday, 10th October, the day of the meeting, showed certain influences we should be aware of and alerted us to certain matters to do with our work. With Saturn at the bottom of the chart, someone was trying to undermine the group and its participation in the story in which we were all taking part.

The different groups then discussed the clearing work they had been doing. Jean, together with others, had collected a ring from a local church. Julia spoke about clearing a Sacred King site with Mary. Mary spoke about the Dragon lines she is finding. One is local and one in Cornwall, in or around Tintagel. Tups and Jenny in Norfolk had cleared Sea Henge, which had recently been very much in the news. English Heritage had removed the wood circle "in order to preserve it". Tups had felt a huge energy during the clearing. She saw the circle restored at the etheric level. Robert said that there were significant planetary changes after the work done at Avebury and Sea Henge. If enough people come together, they can change the destiny of Humankind and Nature.

At the meeting on 15 August of that year Robert had said we would reach the Mines of Moria - a former great kingdom of the dwarves but now abandoned and desolate - before Christmas. Today, Sunday 10th October, when Robert's talk had ended, the Nine Walkers congregated for a cup of tea in the conservatory, which was light and airy with magnificent views. We started to discuss the journey through the Mines of Moria when Robert stood up and walked decisively across the room, his eyes fixed on an unseen point and said: "We have just gone through the Mines of Moria".

It is hardly surprising that the terrifying journey through the Mines, through the endless dark, twisting passages, should have taken place with Robert present, in his role of Gandalf. Only Gandalf knew the way and without his guidance and the dim light, which shone from the tip of his staff as the only source of light, the Company would never have made it through. For that moment at least the conservatory had been the lofty hall of the dwarves. Robert had earlier told Caroline she was to be in charge of the Nine at the mines of Moria. This accords with the story, for Aragorn had to take Gandalf's place as leader after Gandalf was lost to them in his confrontation with the Balrog, a fiery, evil creature of great power. Long ago the mines were abandoned because the workings of the dwarves had gone too deep and disturbed this ancient evil from the Old World. So that part of the story had been interfaced – mercifully by Robert – and then communicated to us.

Fittingly, therefore, he then announced that this was the last meeting of the year. We all of us had plenty to be getting on with over the winter months and would carry on with our clearing work when the occasion arose, whilst at the same time continuing to be aware of our parts in the continuing story of the Ring.

Chapter 32

Fisherton Mill

The following day, Monday 11th October, Cassie suggested that we should have lunch at a rather unusual place called Fisherton Mill, a large, former mill converted to a space for artists to sell their work, and also a restaurant. There were some sculptures outside in the forecourt and, as the weather was so mild, we ate outside.

That evening, as Cassie was driving with one of her daughters to a school musical evening, they saw in the sky at the roundabout a cloud which resembled an enormous eagle with wings outstretched. Had anyone else noticed the unmistakable image of an eagle if they too had looked up whilst waiting in the traffic? Remembering that the battle of the Pellenor Fields had not long ago taken place at Avebury, she noted that it appeared to be flying west which led her to conclude that it was one of the great Eagles who came flying from the land of Mordor to Minas Tirith, bearing the tidings of the great victory of the Lords of the West. Frodo, the Ring-bearer, had fulfilled his Quest and the Ring had been cast into Mount Doom. The realm of Sauron was ended and the battle had been won.

Turning off the roundabout to go north, she received confirmation of this as she saw in the distance an immense dark cloud rising high in the sky edged with a brilliant gold light. This reminded her of the black cloud which rose from the wreckage of the Dark Tower – "a vast soaring darkness sprang into the sky, flickering with fire". It was the spirit of Sauron leaving the earth. She knew then that this was indeed the eagle, which brought the tidings of Sauron's defeat to Minas Tirith. We could hardly bring ourselves to believe this, as there were many other parts of the story that we had not yet experienced. However, Robert had always told us that our experiences would not necessarily be in sequence and, when we contacted him, he confirmed that the battle had indeed been won, but only at one level; there were other levels at which it had to be waged. This dampened our rejoicing a little, but not much.

In the papers the following day there was the picture of an eagle, which supposedly, on its annual migration from central Russia to Africa, had landed instead in the Scilly Isles. This was due to the work our group had done on the earth's magnetic lines at Avebury the previous week, and the eagle had consequently lost its bearings. It was also, of course, the Universe echoing the flight of the great Eagle.

Two days later we both decided that, as it was another sunny autumn day, we would get out of the house, have lunch again at Fisherton Mill and then visit Heale Gardens in the Woodford Valley, which was open to the public. The gardens bordering the river Avon were peaceful and beautiful and, as we wandered over the lawns by the river, we realised we were in Ithilien where Frodo and Sam were healed of their hurts after their terrible ordeal at Mount Doom. We came across a gardener picking off the heads of the lavender, a herb with healing properties, and as we walked down a long avenue, as Frodo and Sam had done, we felt that Heale Garden was truly a place of healing.

Strangely, we had lunch at Fisherton Mill for a third time on the Saturday and realised, at last, why we kept returning. We had missed all the signs we should have been noticing. In the forecourt, where we were again able to sit outside for lunch, were two large sculptures. One was in wood and showed two men holding a plank of wood at either end, with one of the men holding the end up and the other crouching and holding it down, rather like a seesaw. The other was in metal and showed the earth in the form of a hollowed out globe lying at an angle of forty-five degrees composed of slender strips of metal and an arrow with a golden head and feathers piercing it. Round the band of metal in the middle were written various capitals of the world and the different time zones. There were also small sculptures of animals such as two cockerels in intricate metalwork.

The symbolism of the two men shows the two Sacred Kings, in their different roles, one supreme and the other as second-best, but jealously biding his time. It could also represent the 'old' King crouching, on his way out, as he gives way to the 'young' King standing over him, taking his place. The cockerel in the pagan

163

cults was identified with the Sacred King for it was sacred to Apollo, the Sun God. The two cockerels, therefore, echo the sculpture of the men: one perched on a step looking down on the other. Cats are sacred to the Goddess and in front of the two men there was a carving of a large wooden cat: it represents the Queen who ruled supreme in the name of the Goddess during this cult.

The sculpture of the world represents many things but here, primarily, we think it shows that the cult of the Sacred King was world-wide, but the golden arrow represents hope - hope that the bringing into human consciousness of this hidden trauma will heal the wounds and enable humankind to go forward into a new dispensation, a new way of life for which every being on earth on the side of the Forces of Light so deeply longs.

In a corner of the courtyard and up some steps was a rather overgrown area. It consisted of a small pond badly in need of attention, with a few goldfish and a defunct fountain. There were a couple of sculptures: an anchor and a semi-abstract sculpture of a man and a woman representing the opposites, a construct which will cease in this new Age when the pairs of opposites, male and female, Light and Dark, will be resolved. The whole area had an air of neglect. The Piscean Age as represented by the name "Fisherton", the water, the anchor, had ended and, as we stood silently there, we realised that this corner was a symbol of something that was decayed and dead. Indeed, the end of an Age.

In this context, we then wondered about the significance of the sculpture of the two rival kings, who dominated the courtyard. We realised how the competitive spirit aroused in the two men came to taint society and we felt it was suggesting that this spirit would soon be at an end.

There was an amusing sequel to this when we returned to Fisherton Mill for a small celebratory lunch with Cassie's father on her and Caroline's birthdays in December 1999 (we were born on the same day). After looking at the menu for some time, we all chose the fish. It looked delicious when it arrived at the table and for a while we chewed away wondering if the rather strange taste was the Thai spices in which it had been marinated or, horrors, was the fish 'off'? After a little while Caroline suddenly announced, "I think this fish is definitely 'off'. What about yours?" At which both Cassie and Edwin also realised for certain that their fish was also bad. We called the waiter who kindly gave us replacements. Before leaving, we spoke to the chef who was puzzled in the extreme. He had bought the fish the day before from his usual, reliable source and it had been marinating in the refrigerator overnight before being cooked the following day. It was not until at least a fortnight later that we suddenly realised the significance of this incident. The Piscean Age had passed and the Fish was not only dead, it was decaying! The timing was immaculate as everyone was gearing up for the nationwide Millenium celebrations less than three weeks away.

As we have so often experienced during the reworking of *Ring Quest*, when completing a particular topic, we experienced a synchronicity. On the day we made the above revisions, in fact, minutes after writing the above, a friend called by to pick up a book Cassie was lending her for her holiday. She carried a pair of brand new, black Doc Marten boots, which none of her menfolk wanted and so she was taking them to a charity shop. On an impulse she wondered if Cassie might have a use for them. Cassie picked them up and saw something shining in one of the shoes. It was a new watch. Her friend then remembered that she was also giving away the watch, as she couldn't read the face. The meaning of this singular experience is that it is confirming that the old Time/Age is dead – the shoe was black – but a new Age has been born –the new watch. The shoe is of great significance in the Cult of the Sacred King where, in some interpretations of the cult, his foot – and leg – were held to be the particularly sacred parts of his body. It is from this memory that foot and shoe fetishism stem. A shoe or boot, which had been worn by the Sacred King was believed to have extraordinary powers of virility and fertility. Therefore the black Doc Marten has the 'power' to give birth to the New 'Time' after the death of the Age of the Fish.

A hangover from those times is to be seen in portraits of Kings in full regalia. One stockinged leg is prominently revealed from the folds of the ermine cloak in an elegantly heeled shoe so that the sacred heel might not touch the ground. Or there are portraits of the King seated on his throne, exposing just the one leg but this time with the sacred foot resting on a stool so that it does not touch the ground.

It is interesting to note that the headquarters of the powerful Mayor of London are located in the leg and paw of the Lion outline in London. It further proves how the energy of kingship has been corrupted by the Cult of the Sacred King.

Chapter 33

The Earth Sign of the Bull

It was not until February of 2000 that we cleansed the One Ring in the element of 'earth' for the first time. Some months ago we had located the outline of Taurus the Bull. Studying the names of the streets we noticed the word Oseney Crescent in Kentish Town, just to the north of The Twins. We realised that the Crescent resembled an eye and that 'Oseney' sounded very much like 'oxen eye'. Could this be 'the Bull's eye we wondered? Focusing now on the roads enclosing both the streets and the Crescent we could quite distinctly make out the head of the bull and we could see that the eye was located in exactly the right spot within it. We then noticed that the continuation of the road, which formed the top of the head, bent at just the right angle to form the horns of a bull. To cap it all, at the centre of the crescent eye was a church. At that point we felt we had found the site where the Ring should be cleansed. The eye was a big clue that this was an energy point and the church was further confirmation. This time we secured the site instantly.

Robert had finally suggested that we should cleanse the Ring in accordance with the seasons. Thus we should cleanse it in the element of fire in the summer, in water in spring, in air in the Autumn and in earth in the winter. Such knowledge would have been natural to the pagan peoples such as the Celts. On hearing it, it seemed so obvious and logical. Yet, as we had not thought to synchronise with the living world we are a part of, it was just another example of how, as Robert tells us, we have lost our connection with that world. We need to move away from belief systems to a living reality.

So it was on 3 February 2000, having found out that the One Ring had reconstituted itself again, we set off to collect it and then cleanse it in the element of earth. It was a suitably wintry day, one of those flat, dark grey days in London. The weather was surprisingly mild but the branches of trees and shrubs were bare and stark.

We had chosen to retrieve the Ring at St Martin's in the Fields, partly because it was next to The National Gallery and we wanted to see the Botticelli Exhibition to look at his painting of *The Mystic Nativity*. We looked round the exhibition, had lunch in the basement café and made our way to the church. Having safely summoned the Ring, we decided to take the Underground as the Northern Line took us straight to Kentish Town from where our destination was a short walk. Caroline then had an unpleasant experience on the train so that we rather regretted this decision.

Just one stop before we were due to get off, a very bold-looking girl dressed all in black with black hair and ostentatiously chewing gum sat immediately opposite her, even though all the seats on the Other Side of the carriage were empty. Sensing that this was no ordinary person she silently challenged her but she did not move away. Realising that the Other Side had sent someone stronger than herself, she avoided her gaze for as long as she could but suddenly found herself catching her eye, whereupon the woman gave her a nasty stare. Caroline had been meticulous in protecting herself and apart from feeling annoyed, she did not feel she had been harmed, which Robert later confirmed. Cassie had also been aware of a menacing feeling coming from the woman but had not realised she was from the Other Side.

Taurus is a sign connected to the good, solid material things of life and the area, which is once more coming up in the world, consists of large, solid Victorian houses. As we approached the church in Oseney Crescent we saw that it was almost derelict and surrounded by scaffolding which appeared to be holding it up rather than for repair purposes. We reached the gate and there, as at the lake in Regent's Park and as if waiting for us, was a grey squirrel. It whisked away round the side of the church with us following, scratched a little in some earth and ran off. We took this as an indication of the exact spot where we were to purify the Ring. Opening up the white handkerchief we carefully tipped the Ring on to the earth, asking for it to be cleansed in the element of earth in the astrological sign of the Bull.

That evening there was a programme on television about a super-volcano under Yellowstone Park in Wyoming in the United States, which is showing ominous signs of erupting. According to the geologists, the volcano erupts on a 600,000-year cycle, and this last happened 640,000 years ago. The next eruption is therefore long overdue. It would have devastating effects on climate plunging the northern hemisphere into a volcanic winter for years to come. As we had that day cleansed the Ring in the element of Earth, this seemed a significant

TAURUS ~ *the Bull*

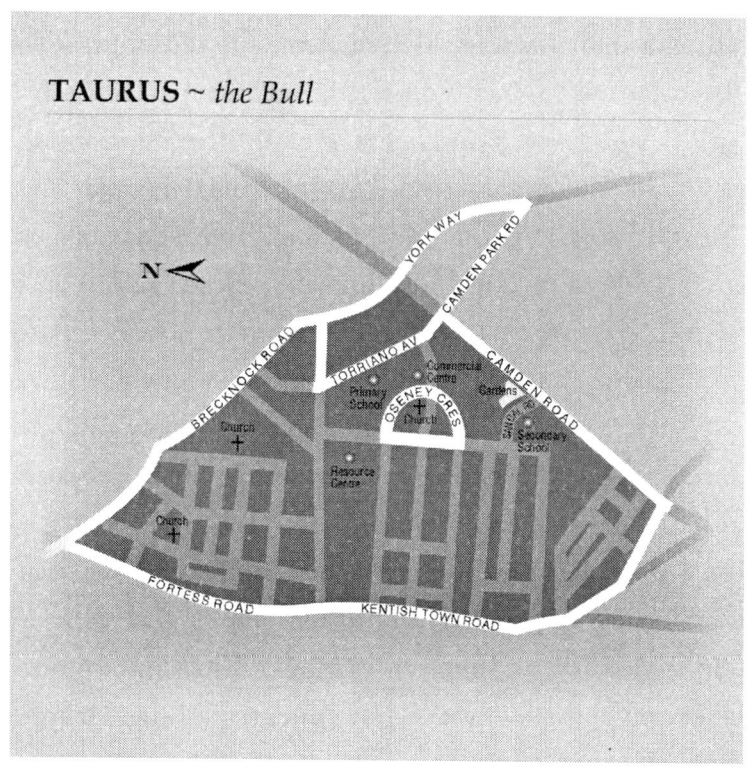

synchronicity. When we had cleansed the Ring in Air its effect had been on the realm of ideas and therefore politics. In Earth the effect would be on the natural, physical world. Fearful that, somehow, we might have set something off, we spoke to Robert about it and heaved a sigh of relief when he said that, on the contrary, things had been 'settled down'. That made us think. We began to understand more fully that by interacting with another dimension and changing the pattern at that level, it had an immediate effect on the physical world – for the better.

Chapter 34

The Royal Line

Meanwhile, experiences mirroring Aragorn's continued. Exactly a week after our visit to London to cleanse the Ring in earth Caroline had a dream, one of those "real" dreams, where she was exerting all her power against some foe. After what seemed a very long time, the danger was over and she was able to relax. On waking she immediately thought of the Palantir, the 'Seeing' stone, which Aragorn had wrested from Sauron. She told Robert about it and he warned that she should put it safely away – at the etheric level - at once! Feeling silly that she hadn't realised this herself, she wrapped it carefully in a silken scarf and put it in a safe place.

About the same time, neighbours offered to cut the top branches of an old pear tree hanging over the garden wall. We brought two of the branches into the house, which, surprisingly, broke into white blossom a week later. It struck us that they were branches from the White Tree, Telperion, symbol of the Royal Line. The two branches represented the two 'branches' of the Royal Line,[16] which were united in the marriage of Arwen and Aragorn, thus guaranteeing the continuation of the Royal Line.

On 12 April Caroline moved house, temporarily renting a cottage. The cottage was part of a complex of converted stables and barns called *King's Stables* and, as she walked through the gate, she looked up at the cupola with the royal crest, the Lion and the Unicorn and saw for the first time the inscription, "Long Live the King 1910 – 1935", commemorating George V's Silver Jubilee. This mirrors the scene in *The Lord of the Rings* where Aragorn, crowned king outside the city gates of Minas Tirith, enters the city after a lapse of a thousand years to claim his inheritance as heir to the royal line of Numenor. Even stranger in its implications, and startling proof that the story of *The Lord of the Rings* is being re-enacted at this moment in humankind's history, was the fact that, on taking over the cottage on that day, she did not immediately move in as her furniture was still in store and could not be brought out for another six weeks. She eventually moved in the middle of May 2000. Like Aragorn, she had entered the city, but did not take up her abode there until later. A final touch - in the middle of the village there was an ancient, long distance route called *Monarch's Way*.

At Christmas 2000, we had a last reflection of the Story on the physical plane that year. The family had decided to attend Midnight Mass at the parish church and, on the way there, someone remembered that Madonna and Guy Ritchie were spending their honeymoon with friends, Sting and his wife, Trudie, in the valley and wondered if they would be at the service. Most of us thought they wouldn't. However, we were wrong. Not long after we had taken our seats in the tiny, crowded church we noticed a group sitting in the choir stalls which, much to our surprise, included Madonna and Guy. We think it is apparent to

174

most people that famous pop stars are the new royalty and Madonna and Guy with their daughter and newly born baby son were, at that moment, representing the King and Queen with their young family. And perhaps the word 'Madonna' is telling us that the Holy Family is of the same royal line as Aragorn and Arwen.

Conclusion

The Millenium seems a good point at which to end this book. Tolkien's, *The Lord of the Rings,* is being re-enacted in the here and now. A Fellowship has been formed to match the original Fellowship and our Quest is well underway. We have successfully found sites with sufficient power to cleanse the Ring belonging to the Dark Lord in each of the elements in which the Ring was forged – fire, water, air and earth. Cleansing the Ring was ongoing for we had learnt that it exists at different levels, going back through time. To date, we have only cleansed it at one of those levels.

When we set out on the Quest we had little idea that the theme of royalty was going to be so important as, initially, the focus seemed to be on the One Ring and of the need to 'unmake' it. This had also seemed the major focus in Tolkien's Story. The Fellowship is formed to help Frodo fulfil the task laid upon him by The Council, which is to throw the One Ring into the fire of Mount Doom. However, the importance of the restoration of the King is revealed towards the end when, much to almost everybody's surprise, Aragorn turns out to be the heir to the throne of Gondor. Gandalf passes the stewardship of Middle Earth to Aragorn saying that it is now for him, as King, to order the New Age of Man. Is it any wonder that Sauron/the Dark Lord so strenuously sought the destruction of the King and the Royal Line?

Sauron's successors have continued to seek the death of the King and to undermine or destroy the Royal Line through Time. We found out just how successful 'they' have been in this aim with the discovery of the existence, in our past, of the Cult of Sacrifice of the King. Much of the evidence of this terrible practice has been destroyed and/or suppressed, partly as a result of the King's own fear. We have only been left with the peripheral pieces and the fallout. With this in mind, we should be less surprised that the Royal theme was proving to be of such importance on this Quest.

New elements were to come into our journey of which, at this stage, we were as yet unaware. These will appear in the next book. We learn more about how Man must travel back the way he came. This means raising our vibrations in order to access a higher level. And we learn, with Robert's help, how this might be achieved.

APPENDIX I

Sir Gawain and the Green Knight

In the Arthurian legend, on New Year's Day a very tall and immensely powerful man on horseback enters King Arthur's great feasting hall. What astonishes all the knights and ladies gathered there is that his armour, his clothes and his skin are a vivid shade of green. He bears a huge battleaxe. Addressing the assembly courteously, he says that he just wants to play a New Year pastime. The man of greatest prowess at the Court of King Arthur is to strike one blow against him with his mighty axe on condition that he, the Green Knight, is allowed to reciprocate the blow a year and a day later at a pre-arranged place of the Green Knight's choosing.

There are no immediate volunteers but in the end Sir Gawain takes up the challenge. He raises the Green Knight's mighty axe and cuts off his head with one blow. Blood spouts everywhere. Then, to the amazement of all present, the headless Green Knight stands up, picks up his head, which then begins to speak, reiterating that he expects to meet with Sir Gawain a year and a day hence, at a small chapel in the woods.

The year passes and, reluctantly, Sir Gawain sets off for his meeting with the Green Knight at the Green Chapel. He reaches a castle on Christmas Eve close by the Chapel where he is welcomed by the Lord and Lady and given hospitality. After three days, having resisted the overtures of the Lord's beautiful wife, Sir Gawain sets out to meet the Green Knight.

He finds him whetting the blade of an axe in readiness for the fight. As arranged, the Green Knight moves to behead Gawain, but only strikes him on the third axe-swing, barely cutting his neck. The Green Knight then reveals himself as Sir Gawain's recent host. He spares Sir Gawain's life and explains that he has passed the tests set him.

'The Beheading Game' features widely in Celtic myth and it clearly has its origin in that earlier period of history when the Sacred King was sacrificed at that time of year – the midwinter solstice – and beheaded. The pagan custom has been replaced with the Christian festival of Christmas, celebrating the birth of Jesus or the 'New' King who took the place of the 'Old' King. However, the memory of that terrifying end lived on for a long time.

The purpose of theatre is often to make us confront our fears and then see the story changed to offer a happy ending. This reassures and helps to re-educate the subconscious mind. So it is with 'The Beheading Game.' The cruel and barbaric practice, reserved solely for men of royal or noble birth, is turned into a 'mere Christmas pastime', at which everyone can laugh light-heartedly. In the original poem, great emphasis is placed on the Beheading Game being fun and frivolous. This way many men's fear was kept under control. Subconsciously, it would have been a huge relief for those of King Arthur's knights who had once been Sacred Kings themselves, to see Sir Gawain return unscathed from his ordeal.

APPENDIX II

The Sun's Journey

The origins of the Cult of Sacrifice of the Sacred King are to be found in sun worship, hence the sacrifice of the King at the summer and winter solstices. The Egyptians believed from the earliest times that 'God is the hidden Being, and no man hath known his form', but the Sun-god Ra was 'the visible emblem and the type and symbol of God who was worshipped in prehistoric times'. He rose every morning, born of his mother, and travelled across the sky in the Atet boat until noon as the sun rose to its zenith. From noon, as the sun declined, Ra continued his celestial voyage in the Sektet boat and was received into the arms of the goddess as the Sun sank below the horizon. Cassie came across a number of beautiful hymns in honour of the Sun-god Raw, taken from the oldest copies of the *Book of the Dead*, in a book called *Egyptian Religion* by E.A. Wallis who was one time Keeper of the Egyptian and Assyrian Antiquities in the British Museum. The following composition, part hymn and part prayer, is taken from the Papyrus of Ani from the *Book of the Dead*:

> 'A hymn of praise to thee, O thou who risest like unto gold, and who dost flood the world with light on the day of thy birth. Thy mother giveth thee birth, and straightway thou dost give light upon the path of (thy) Disc, O thou great Light who shinest in the heavens. Thou makest the generations of men to flourish through the Nile-flood, and thou dost cause gladness to exist in all lands, and in all cities...thou who art glorious in Majesty in the Sektet boat, and most mighty in the Atet boat! (The Sun's evening and morning boats)...when thou risest in the horizon of heaven, a cry of joy cometh forth to thee from the mouth of all peoples thou beautiful Being, thou dost

181

renew thyself in thy season in the form of the Disk within thy mother Hathor..Hail, god of life, thou lord of love, all men live when thou shinest; thou art crowned king of the gods. The goddess Nut doeth homage unto thee, and the goddess Maat embraceth thee at all times. Thou goest forth each day over heaven and earth, and art made strong each day by thy mother Nut...Ra liveth in Maat the beautiful...Isis and Nephthys salute thee, they sing unto thee songs of joy at thy rising in the boat, they protect thee with their hands.'

When she first read this she was struck by its remarkable similarity in form to the ideas behind the Cult of the Sacred Sun King of the pagan cults. She was especially struck by the way the day was divided in two when the God Ra changed boats after the sun had reached its height at mid-day. This corresponded with the one Sacred King representing the waxing sun and his twin replacing him at mid-summer who embodied the waning sun. The idea that the sun is 'born' from the Goddess at the beginning of the day and received by her at day's end when it sinks below the horizon compares with the idea of the Sacred Sun King also being reborn from the Goddess the day after the winter solstice having been received back into her womb when the sun was sun 'died' at mid-winter.

In the hymn, the protective and nurturing love of the goddesses for Ra is very moving, particularly in the way they protect him with their hands. However, if we imagine a shift in the balance of power in favour of the Feminine, we can begin to understand how the Sun King became subordinate to the all-creative power of the Goddess from whom he had his being. As the personification of the Sun, it becomes a hideously logical step to sacrifice the King in order to benefit from those wonderful life-giving powers which were believed to be stored in his very body.

When the Sun God Ra sank beneath the horizon, it was believed he traversed the underworld before being given birth again from the womb of the Goddess Hathor. One of Ra's titles was Lord of the Underworld. Egyptian texts describe the passage of the sun through the underworld during the night and its dangers are not dissimilar to the horrors of the Christian Hell with 'the river of fire, the pits of fire, the snake and the scorpion' (E.A. Wallis Budge. *Egyptian Religion*). We find the same Lord of the Underworld in Celtic mythology.

Egyptian sun worship spread to the Mediterranean countries via Crete with whom it traded. Robert Graves tells us in his book, *The White Goddess,* how bands of Mediterranean peoples were driven out of their own countries by Kings who had overthrown the Queen/Goddess whom they replaced with an all-powerful Father God. Those driven out made their way to Britain taking their religious practices with them. Certainly, we discovered through our clearing work that the greatest numbers of sacrificed Kings were to be found in the south. It is on Britain's southern shores that those fleeing worshippers of the Goddess would have originally landed.

The Sun Warrior

In the course of her research Cassie came across the 'solar hero' and it became clear that his origins are to be found in the former Cult of the Sacrifice of the Sun King. He is a well-known figure in stories from our ancient oral tradition, which we call myth which, as many know, go way back into the mists of time.

The Irish solar hero, Lugh of the Long Arm and the Arthurian Sir Gawain, nephew of King Arthur of Camelot, are just two examples. Their astounding strength is clearly linked with that of the sun in the tales.

When the Irish folk hero, Lugh of the Long Arms and his men approach the great assembly on the Hill of Usna in the county of Erin, they are described as: 'a stately band of warriors, all mounted on white steeds, coming towards them from the east; and at their head, high in command over all, rode a young champion, tall and comely, with a countenance as bright and glorious as the setting sun.' On another occasion as Lugh approaches the Formorian enemy, one of them watching Lugh approaching from the West says 'A wonderful thing has come to pass this day; for the sun, it seems to me, has risen in the west'. A druid replies 'The light you see is the brightness of the face...of Lugh of the Long Arms, our deadly enemy'.

In single combat with Sir Lancelot, Sir Gawain is described as having a strength which increased as the sun climbed to its highest point in the sky at noon, and then that super-human strength leaves him as the sun begins its descent: 'Then had Sir Gawain such a grace and gift that an holy man had given to him, that every day in the year, from undern till high noon, his might increased those three hours as much as thrice his strength. And then when it was past noon Sir Gawain had no more but his own might' (*Le Morte d'Arthur* by Sir Thomas Malory).

By endowing these two heroes with the qualities of the Sacred Sun King, the storytellers of the day were wishing to impress upon their audience the exceptional prowess of the hero and his superiority over other men. Even though the Cult had been ruthlessly suppressed, certain charismatic aspects of it were kept alive, particularly if they enhanced the standing of a champion so that the enemy would fear him. Perhaps in those far off times it was not long in the past that the king had been sacrificed, as the Cult continued to be practised in more remote areas long after its practice had ceased elsewhere. The audience would have understood the allusion to the Sacred King who had been a demi-God, and they would have been in awe of a hero given the attributes of the Sun King.

Another story concerns the Irish Cuchulain, who was Lugh's son. The ruling Queen Maeve sets off for Ulster with her army to capture the famed White-horned Bull of Connaught, which she covets. She carefully chooses a particular time of the year when a spell, laid upon her enemy by an angry goddess many years ago, strikes the warriors of the Red Branch of Ulster: 'That for a certain season each year, as winter was beginning, they would lose all their strength, become as helpless as new-born babes, and fall into a deep sleep.'

This physical weakness that mysteriously overtakes these warriors or heroes alludes to those former days of the pagan Cult when it was believed that the King became 'old', and therefore weak, at the onset of winter. This reflected the growing weakness of the sun which people could feel at that time of year as the weather became cooler. It therefore became 'old' and 'died' at the winter solstice. (*Old Celtic Romances* by P.W. Joyce).

The Head

Archaeological evidence also points to the existence of the Cult of the Sacred King. A third century Celtic sanctuary discovered at Ribemont-sur-Ancre in the north of France, near the Somme, held one of the largest collections skulls and human bones to be found in Gaul. It is 800 metres long and stacked with the skulls and arm and leg bones of 1000 individuals aged between fifteen and twenty years. Their skulls were detached and specially 'treated'. The narrow age range and youth of the victims point to a ritual death. One explanation as to why this cult has been so comprehensively erased from history, is that it stands to reason that when the King finally overthrew the Queen he destroyed all reminders of his terrible past, including gruesome sanctuaries such as the one which survived at Ribemont-sur-Ancre. (*The Celts: First Masters of Europe* by Christiane Elurere).

Excavations carried out at Danebury Iron-Age hill fort in Wiltshire by Barry Cunliffe and recorded in his book *Danebury*, states, 'human skulls were found in eight ritual pits: six were adult males, one was female and one of a child.' The author goes on to suggest that human sacrifice could not be ruled out. On the bronze door kept at the State Historical Museum in Stockholm sacrificial pits are shown filled with bearded, warrior heads and severed hands and arms.

In Celtic mythology there is a direct connection between the Goddess and the severed head. After the slaughter of battle, the heads of the enemy were stuck on what was called the Pole of Macha the Red - the name given to the battle aspect of the Great Queen in Ireland. In the Hindu religion the Goddess of Death and Regeneration, Kali, is shown holding the lotus symbol of regeneration in one hand and wearing a necklace of human skulls.

In many cultures throughout the world, such as that in Indonesia, the people were at one time 'head hunters'. On the island of Borneo, the head was cradled in the laps of women and talked to, as it was believed such behaviour encouraged it to make the crops fertile. Such behaviour makes a direct connection with the fertilising powers of the sun. (*The White Goddess*, Robert Graves).

The belief in the power of the head of a great champion persisted even after the Cult had died out. The Roman writer, Diodurus Siculus, as he travelled through Celtic Gaul, describes heads being nailed to the victor's house to show off his valour. He records that they might: 'soak the heads of their most illustrious enemies in cedar oil and keep them carefully in a chest and show them off to strangers, each priding himself that for one or other of these heads, either a forebear or his father or he himself, had refused to take a large sum of money'.

A survival from the days of the pagan cult is the custom of rolling a large cheese down a hill on Whit Monday at Cooper's Hill, Birdlip in Gloucestershire. As it gains speed local boys chase after it in order to catch it and claim the prize. Clearly, this practice would originally have taken place at midsummer. The large, round, yellow cheese represents the sun beginning its downward trajectory to the midwinter solstice after having reached its highest point in the sky. We can speculate that at one time it was the King's head which was sent rolling down the hill and the cheese is a substitute. To have been the possessor of the head of the King with its marvellous fertilising and healing properties would have been a prize indeed. Evidently, the people believed so strongly in the beneficial powers of this ritual that they kept alive the practice.

186

In other parts of Britain, flaming barrels or a flaming sun wheel, are rolled downhill in commemoration of this once most important of pagan, religious festivals. Until recently, on Midsummer Eve the villagers of Leusdon, Devon, would roll a flaming cartwheel down the slopes of nearby Mel Tor. (*Mysterious Britain*, Janet and Colin Bord).

After the ritual sacrifice of the King, his head was often taken to a strategic site where it could detect an enemy from afar. (This fits in with what Robert told us about the King taking an oath to defend the land from enemies.) In the Welsh Hero Tale, King Bran is mortally wounded in a fierce fight against the Irish to avenge their ill-treatment of his sister, Branwen. After the battle he bids his friends to cut off his head and tells them to: 'Take my head and return to Britain. Carry it to London and bury it on the White Mount at Tower Hill with the face towards France. So long as it remains buried there no enemy shall invade Britain from over the sea.' (*Hero Tales from the British Isles* by Barbara Leonie Picard).

Later, with the advent of Christianity and the desire to do away with the old customs, King Arthur dug up Bran's head at the White Mount at the Tower of London for he declared: 'It was right that the land of Britain should owe its freedom to the courage of its living men, and not to the magical powers of a dead king's head.' (*Hero Tales from the British Isles* by Barbara Leonie Picard).

For those living on the south coast the greatest danger of attack came from the sea, so they would have set the King's head on a promontory. This is the most likely origin of so many vantage points or headlands, having the word 'head' in their name such as: in Dorset, Durlston Head, St Alban's Head and Beer Head. In Cornwall and Devon we find Gribbin Head, Pencarrow Head, Rame Head, Bolt Head, Scabbacombe Head, and Berry Head.

In 1988 Cassie and her daughters spent a week's holiday with a friend in a rented cottage in Dorset, in the village of Shipton Gorge, not far from the sea. They visited the Dorchester Museum and she was very interested to come across two large, crudely carved stone heads with the description: 'Two supposedly Celtic heads found built into walls at Shipton Gorge.' It occurred to her that these heads had been positioned there to ward off invaders at that weak point in the natural defences of the coastline. As the name says, the village was in a gorge created by a river flowing through it and down to the sea, which had made a break in the cliffs. There was a good sandy beach, which an invading force could have used for landing their boats before working their way inland up the gorge.

A final thought, we have many expressions which include the word 'head' which are very likely to have originated from this Cult, such as 'Keep your head on', 'He has a good head on his shoulders', or 'Heads will roll'. Corporations, businesses, schools, etc., all have the word 'Head' for their leaders, just as the King was the tribe's titular 'head'.

As ever, when Cassie was about to start writing the chapter on the importance of the 'head' of the Sacred King eight years' ago, she experienced a synchronicity. She happened to read The Daily Mail (Thursday, July 8 1999) and Mac's cartoon for the day showed a hospital bed with only the patient's head sitting on the sheet which was very much alive, and looking surprised. A surgeon and nurse were standing by the bedside and the surgeon was thanking this liberal-minded patient for kindly having donated so many parts of his body; so many it appears, that he had only been left with his head.

APPENDIX III

Clearing Energy Sites

When clearing a site of negativity, the first thing to do is protect yourself. Basically, you need to ground and balance. A thought of protection is good enough or you can visualise a light bubble of protection, or some other image. A minimum of two people is advisable and, preferably, more as you will then be able to work more powerfully and safely together.

It is not only Sacred King sites that need clearing. Reading the local history of an area will perhaps throw up other traumatic incidents such as battles, murders and of course, hauntings. Once the site is known, quickly secure it by encircling it with light or by putting your hand on a map. You do not even need to go to a site. You can imagine yourselves there and that will take you there. Stand, preferably in the centre, in a circle holding hands and keep it simple. Tune in to your intuition. We like to sound the 'Aum', sometimes harmonising and sometimes clashing, on purpose. Robert always says your own words are best. If it is a site where the King was sacrificed, draw in more of the golden light for healing, as sacrifice is a misuse of the feminine energy so balance needs to be restored. You then request the Kings to ask to be released from the oath they swore to their Liege Lord, the preceding King, to defend the Land. You do not have to be a medium to do this: it is sufficient to direct your thought to them. You can call on angels or their loved ones to help guide them. You may also like to ask for help from the nature spirits who, Robert says, have been pushed out by humanity to the outer margins between the worlds.

If clearing a battlefield you can draw in more of the silver light as warfare is a misuse of the masculine energy. At all sites, ask for all trapped sentient beings to be released. Then cleanse the earth and balance the energies.

As for recognising Sacred King sites, this is often made easy as Roman Christianity took over many of the pagan sites of worship.

They could not stop people visiting those ancient sites so they appropriated them, and as we know, so many were polluted. You will find that such sites are inevitably on a high point or in marshy land or near water. The ancient origin of the choice of these energy sites is that the masculine energy lines ran through the high points and the feminine ran near water and marshland. You may also find such sites marked by castles, iron-age hill forts, long barrows, stone circles and palaces or grand country houses. They are part of a worldwide energy system set up to try and prevent the earth's energies falling ever lower.

Having made the intention to go and clear a site, look out for the universe responding to you with hints, signs and synchronicities. Afterwards, look out for changes for the better in the area.

While revising the above, we had occasion to ask Robert about clearing sites and we pass on his reply:

'ref to clearing sites – yes it is a continual job.
We clear a site and it is clear:
1. Someone else knows about the energies of the sites and restarts it again
2. This happens time and time again because of books, media, people talking and so on
3. Even the great masters cleared as they went – but it did not, does not last – humans are unaware of the continual dross they make
4. Until we attain our godlike energies once again, we still have to clear sites'

We remember Robert once saying that there only needs to be a grain of memory left at a cleared site for the negativity to be revived by the reasons given above. One obvious source whereby sites become re-polluted, are groups who re-enact famous battles.

Perhaps another is tourists visiting historical sites with the past in mind.

APPENDIX IV

Brutus, Trojan Prince

Many know of the sack of Troy by the Greeks in 1185 B.C not least because of the recent film, simply called *Troy,* starring Brad Pitt and Angelina Jolie. The well-known hero Aeneas, along with his father and some followers, managed to escape the burning and sacking. His wanderings after the break-up of the Trojan Empire are also well known, such as how he captured the heart of Queen Dido of Carthage, a kingdom in North Africa. He and his followers are also considered to be the founders of the city that would one day be called Rome. Perhaps less well known is that Aeneas' father, Prince Anchises, was a cousin of King Priam of Troy and therefore of the royal blood. Therefore that blood line came to British shores in the person of Aeneas' grandson, Brutus, who came with a large following. He had been unable to find a home in the Mediterranean basin for his people so had finally taken the radical step of sailing north to this island.

On reading E. O. Gordon's book, *Prehistoric London: Its Mounds and Circles,* we learnt for the first time that the name Britannia derives from the name of Brutus - the word *tan* is the old British or Japhetic term for *land;* Brutannia is therefore Brutus' Land. Furthermore, Brutus founded London in around 1100 B.C. Its location reminded him of his lost homeland, Troy, which was also built on a tidal estuary. For long it was known as Caer Troia, the New Troy, until the local name of one of the four sacred mounds in London, The Llandin (Parliament Hill), proved more popular.

We are not the only ones to be surprised at how this vital link in British history has been so comprehensively kept under wraps. The tenor of E.O. Gordon's book, as well as that of Isabel Hill Elder's book, *Celt, Druid and Culdee,* is one of deep concern and puzzlement. How did the writings of the old chroniclers and historians come to be dismissed as mere invention and fairytale? They both point out that the old chroniclers of Britain, including

Gildas, Nennius and Geoffrey of Monmouth who compiled the legends of King Arthur and his Round Table, were the most learned men of their day, and were held in high regard. They were patronised by the princes of the land and the chronology of Kings and their actions were meticulously written down. As Milton, author of *Paradise Lost* comments, to paraphrase: 'For the names of successive kings not to have been real persons, nor for them to have at least in some part done what was written they had done, is hard to believe.'

However, put in the context of this book, we should be less puzzled. Ever has the Royal Line been the object of hatred by the Forces of the Left and ever have they striven to wipe it out and destroy all evidence of its existence. What we learnt from E.O. Gordon and Isabel Hill Elder concerning the Royal Line of Brutus and the peoples of these islands in fact turns out to be the opposite of what we had been taught in school. In addition, we find striking comparisons with Tolkien's story.

When the Romans came to the British Isles in AD 43 as children we were taught that the indigenous people were still in a barbaric state. The Romans were greeted by near naked savages coated in a blue paint called woad and brandishing spears. Of course, we have to remember that a great deal of the history that has been taught in British schools has been drawn from Latin sources. They tell us that we owe our civilising influences to Rome. Not so, writes Isabel Hill Elder. Rome owes a great deal to the British. She writes that 'the British, before the arrival of Julius Caesar, were, in all probability, among the most highly educated people on the earth at that time and, as regards scientific research, surpassed both the Greeks and the Romans – a fact testified to by both Greek and Roman writers themselves.'

When Brutus arrived in these islands he did not need to subdue a resistant indigenous people because they were of the same stock. They called themselves the Kymry, or race of Japhet and they were Aryan. Earlier, this People had dispersed far and wide throughout Europe and the near East, including Egypt. E.O. Gordon

193

tells us that Troy was 'regarded as the sacred city of the race of Japhet in the East.'

Instead, Brutus was greeted by his kinsmen, who had come in an earlier migration and were living on Dartmoor. He was taken to the Sacred Mound called Tot Hill from which the present town of Totnes takes its name. There, on the topmost point, called the Gorsedd in Welsh, which means 'Supreme Seat of the Monarch', he was proclaimed Sovereign and King Paramount by the people. E. O. Gordon is at pains to point out that similar artificial Mounds in London - Tothill in Westminster and the Mound at The Tower of London - have always been considered Great Seats of Royalty from time immemorial. It was here that British Kings held their courts and their councils. The ancient Royal Palace of Westminster, which was finally destroyed by fire in the time of Henry VIII, was the favourite residence of Edward the Confessor.

After being proclaimed King, E.O. Gordon relates that it is most probable that Brutus would have been taken directly to the centre of administration of the "Mighty Ones" at Avebury where, 'within the supreme Gorsedd, the chosen of the People was "lifted up" by the Elders to a stone seat according to a most ancient custom of the Kymry'. People came to the crowning of the "elected Sovereign Paramount" from all corners of Britain. It took place within the precincts of the mile-wide stone circle of Avebury, a site of high energy, in the presence of a vast number of people.

The symbolism of the ancient practice of the "lifting up", suggests that the King was seen as having a natural spiritual, mental and physical superiority over his fellow men. Tolkien tells us that Aragorn was also a man with superior gifts and a lifespan three times that of other men. On being unanimously hailed King by all the people outside the ruined gates of Minas Tirith, Aragorn, now the King Elessar, rose and we are given the following description: 'Tall as the sea-kings of old, he stood above all that were near; ancient of days he seemed and yet in the flower of manhood; and wisdom sat upon his brow, and strength and healing were in his hands, and a light was about him.' Richard II was the last king to be "lifted" to the throne beneath which was the Stone of Scone, which was kept at the upper end of Westminster Hall until 1833. It is clear that this was no ordinary royal dynasty.

The arrival of Brutus and his followers, bringing with them a High Kingship, can be compared with the arrival of Elendil and his sons on the shores of Middle Earth. Their homeland, the island of Numenor, which means 'Land of the Star' - for it was shaped like a five-pointed star (see *Unfinished Tales* by J. R. R. Tolkien published posthumously) - had been invaded and destroyed. Like Brutus, Elendil was of the blood royal. Once again a new start was being made.

The ancient texts known as the Welsh Triads describe Brutus as one of the 'Three King Revolutionists of Britain,' because he introduced ancient Trojan Law, the recognition of which 'is said to solve all the peculiarities in British Laws and Usages which would otherwise be wholly inexplicable.' These laws set the British apart from their European neighbours because of their unique liberties and high ideals. Every subject was as free as the King. There were no slaves and everyone was entitled to "Common Rights" which were inalienable. E. O. Gordon states that 'Many of these usages are remarkable for their humane and lofty spirit;' For example, the King was subject to the Voice of the People - hence the maxim: "The Country is higher than the King". This is precisely what took place at the crowning of Aragorn: the People were asked whether they wished him to be their King to which the answer was a resounding 'Yes'. The King Elessar had won his spurs during fifty years of toil and hardship.

Another of the high ideals of the Kymric People, which is particularly relevant today with the rise of Muslim fundamentalism, is that women were held in 'exceptional reverence and honour'. This derived from ancient Accadian law in the land of Sumer in what is now Iraq, which makes woman the equal of man. A woman could also inherit the crown as has proven to be the case in Britain. We find the same law applying on the Island of Numenor in Tolkien's trilogy.

Again, a fact that was new to us was that the early Britons were famous for their outstanding physique and athleticism. The Latin chronicler, Strabo, describes British youths as being six inches taller than the tallest man in Rome and powerfully built. The following description given by Isabel Hill Elder could just as well apply to the tall, hardy, grim Rangers of the North, in *The Lord of The Rings*, who were the remnant of the unmixed Race of Men from Numenor. The Britons 'were patient in pain, toil and suffering, accustomed to fatigue, to bearing hunger, cold and all manner of hardships. Bravery, fidelity to their word, manly independence, love of their national free institutions, and hatred of every pollution and meanness were their noble characteristics.'

The spiritual ideals of the Founding Fathers, enshrined in the American Constitution, can also be compared to the introduction of enlightened laws by Brutus to Britain. So we see that history really does repeat itself through the Ages. As Robert today identifies Minas Tirith as The White House in the United States, perhaps we can see a connection between Numenor, the 'Land of the Star', and the five pointed stars on the American National flag, not to mention the five-sided building known as The Pentagon, Headquarters of the Military Establishment of the USA. Interestingly, one of the four Sacred Mounds in London was called The Penton.

It is interesting to observe that the new impetus in North America did not involve a King. This is because such a person would eventually have attracted the corrupted energy of that institution, so it was best to avoid it altogether. However, deeply embedded in the subconscious of the Western people is a deep desire for just that sort of spiritual leadership. That longing is therefore soon projected on to a family dynasty, which subliminally, fulfils the role of a 'royal family'. Just such a dynasty has been the Kennedy family and we all know how its members appear to have been dogged by ill luck - cursed even.

With Brutus establishing a High Kingship in the White Isles with fair Laws, and the Founding Fathers creating a high minded Constitution for the peoples of the United States of America, we see a link through time with Tolkien's story. For as Legolas the Elf says, there is a prophecy that the Line of Luthien - from which stems the Royal Line of Numenor - will never die. Through repetitions of the cycle of destruction and renewal, that Line is still with us today - although in comparative obscurity - as it was throughout Tolkien's trilogy until the very end of the story.

Bibliography

Bord, Janet and Colin *Mysterious Britain* (London, Thorsons, 1995)

Cunliffe, Barry *Danebury: Anatomy of an Iron-Age Hillfort*

Keatman, Martin & Graham Phillips *The Green Stone* (Neville Spearman, 1983)

Curry, Patrick *Defending Middle-Earth Tolkien: Myth & Modernity* (London, HarperCollins 1998)

Elurere, Christiane *The Celts: First Masters of Europe* (London, Thames and Hudson Ltd, 1992)

Gordon, E.O. *Prehistoric London - Its Mounds and Circles* (London, The Covenant Publishing Co., Ltd., 1932)

Graves, Robert *The White Goddess* (London, Faber and Faber Limited, 1961)

        The Greek Myths (Penguin Books, 1992)

Hill Elder, Isabel *Celt, Druid and Culdee* (1973)

Joyce, P.W. *Old Celtic Romances* (Dublin, The Talbot Press Ltd, 1966 (1879))

Kilby, Clyde *Tolkien and The Silmarillion* (Lion Publishing, 1977)

Malory, Sir Thomas *Le Morte D'Arthur* (London, Penguin Books, 1986)

Miller, Hamish & Paul Broadhurst *The Sun and the Serpent* (Launceston, Pendragon Press, 1989)

Picard, Barbara Leonie *Hero Tales from the British Isles* (Penguin Books Ltd, 1966)

Pipe, Marian *Northamptonshire Ghosts & Legends* (Countryside Books, 1993)

Ross, Anne & Don Robbins *the Life and Death of a Druid Prince* (Rider & Co June 1989

Sutphen, Dick *Finding your Answers Within* (New York, Pocket Books, 1989)

Tolkien, J.R.R. *The Lord of the Rings* (London, Unwin Hyman Limited, 1966)

        The Silmarillion (London, Harper Collins, 1994)

        Unfinished Tales (London, Harper Collins, 1980)

        The Hobbit (London, Harper Collins, 1990)

        Sir Gawain and the Green Knight, Pear and Sir Orfeo (George Allen & Unwin Ltd, 1975)

Toulson, Shirley *The Winter Solstice* (Jill Norman & Hobhouse Ltd, 1981)

Wallis Budge, E.A. *Egyptian Religion* (London, Arkana Paperbacks, 1987 (1899))

Watkins, Alfred *The Ley Hunter's Manual* (The Aquarian Press, 1989)

ENDNOTES

[1] At the end of the Second Age a terrible seven- year battle is waged against Sauron. Finally, Isildur kills Sauron in single combat on the slopes of the volcano and removes the Ring from Sauron's finger. He is urged to throw it then and there into the fires of the volcano but Isildur does not, for his will is quickly dominated by that of the Master Ring, and he finds it too 'fair' to destroy.

[2] When Frodo enters the Forest of Lothlorien where the Elven folk live, he is keenly aware of the change in the atmosphere so that his surroundings seem more alive. There is no stain on that Land which is likened to the World as it was in the First Age, for it is under the power of an Elven Ring. Gandalf tells Aragorn that much will be lost at the end of the Third Age because the world is changing. The Elves will 'fade', i.e. they will become invisible to mortal eyes.

[3] Sauron lost his physical body at the time of the destruction of the island of Numenor long ago at the end of the Second Age. Despite this loss he was still able to interact with the living world in a hideous guise, like the living dead, through the use of Black Magic. In the Third Age he creates the terrifying form of an eye. When the Ring falls into the fire with Gollum, Sauron's spirit leaves the world as a vast, black shape in the sky and we are told that he will never be able to take shape again.

[4] The Seven Stones of Seeing were gifts from the Elves to the Numenoreans. The Stones were brought to Middle Earth by the faithful Numenoreans from over the seas. In the time of the story of the Fellowship of the Ring, the Stones had passed out of living knowledge but we learn that three have survived and are being used in secret by Sauron, Saruman and Denethor, Steward of Minas Tirith.

[5] The powerful men who wore them were subverted and eventually controlled by Sauron's will, all except the dwarves. Only the Three Elven Rings were free as they had been forged in secret without Sauron's knowledge.

[6] In his book *Prehistoric London*, (first published in 1914) E. O. Gordon mentions the other two sacred mounds in the "Port of Londin" as the Llandin – Parliament Hill, and the Penton, both of

which, being natural heights, would have been clearly visible as they rose above the surrounding moors, marshes and watery stretches that surrounded the pre-Christian capital. The Tothill was still standing in the reign of Queen Elizabeth I, as it is mentioned by Norden, topographer of Westminster at the time: "Tootehill Street, lying in the west part of the citie, taketh name of a hill near it which is called Toote-hill, in the great feyld near the street". A map of 1746 shows the Toothill Fields (map of 1746) at the bend in that ancient Causeway, the Horseferry Road.

Other well-known mounds are Silbury Hill, the Montem at Eton, the Windsor Round-Table Mound, the Mound at Oxford, Winton (St. Katherine's Hill, Winchester) and the Tot rearing high beside Totnes. Seventy Tot or Toot Hills are mentioned in Hones' *Year Book*, and many more might be added. He adds Tetbury (a corruption of Tot), Teterton Clee and Doddington Wood in Salop. This last has a height of 122 feet.

In the Welsh language Holy Hills or Mounds are called Gorsedds, which means "The Great Seat or throne of the Monarch". We were at once reminded of the Great Seat on the Hill of Seeing of the High Kings of the West in Tolkien's book. E.O. Gordon describes how far-reaching are the views from the summit of the Gorsedd at Totnes. The Great Seat stands on the highest point of the hill and is enclosed by a stone wall, which has never been roofed, like the Round-Table Mound at Windsor. The mound is artificial with the average dimensions of such "piled up", prehistoric Gorsedds, being 100 feet in diameter at the base, narrowing to about 80 at the top.

It is curious that the word 'Tot' (a sacred mound) should mean 'death' in German. Is it possibly because such sacred high places later became associated with human sacrifice? In Tolkien's story of Middle Earth, a precedent for human sacrifice is to be found in the Temple built by Sauron on the Sacred Heights of Numenor. There, the Faithful – those who were still friends of the Elves - were singled out for sacrifice.

Another point of interest is that Wickliffe, in his translation of the Bible applies the word Tot to Mount Zion (2 Sam.v. 7-9). Please see the Appendix on Brutus, the Trojan Prince.

[7] For sceptics of reincarnation as well as the idea that we can carry the memory of a past life trauma in the subconscious mind, we were very struck by the comment in a book called *Finding Your Answers Within* by the American writer Dick Sutphen. He related that when a past life trauma is triggered, you cannot manufacture those emotions of fear, sorrow or anger.

[8] See Tolkien's *The Silmarillian*

[9] Frodo makes Gollum swear on The Ring that he will be a faithful guide and Gollum is delighted to do so if it means he can stay close to The Ring. But he can only be trusted up to a point as Samwise is only too aware.

[10] Aragorn captured Gollum in the Dead Marshes and because of his slippery ways, treated him harshly on the long journey they had together. No love was lost between them.

[11] There is a parallel in the story. Gollum found the bright eyes of the Elves and the tall Men of Numenor intolerable. Sauron's ambassador at the Gates of Mordor could not long hold Aragorn's eye and the power of the Lady Arwen's gaze pierced Frodo's heart.

[12] By appealing to his vanity, Bilbo had cleverly made the dragon roll over in the hope of finding a weak spot on his gem-encrusted underside. The thrush overhears him telling the dwarves about the bare yellow hollow over the dragon's heart. When all seems lost and the town is in flames, the thrush perches on Bard's shoulder and tells him to wait for the moon to appear and aim for the yellow patch on the dragon's belly with his remaining arrow as the dragon hurtles down on the beleaguered town, bent on total destruction

[13] Beren gave the Silmaril to King Thingol in exchange for his daughter Luthien's hand in marriage. Bilbo gave the Arkenstone to both the Elven King and Bard to use as a bargaining counter in exchange for their rightful share of the dragon's treasure.

[14] The spiritual interpretation of the phenomenon known as "the diamond-ring effect", which occurs at the precise moment that the moon covers the face of the sun at the time of an eclipse, is that it represents Nenya.

[15] As all fled before the black, hooded and cloaked figure, his way was barred by Gandalf sitting silently on the white horse, Shadowfax. He told the Lord of the Nazgul that he could not enter the City. In response, The Lord of the Nazgul laughed mockingly and lifting up his sword, he prepared to engage Gandalf in combat. But at that moment, the cock crowed and from far away could be heard the blowing of a multitude of horns announcing the arrival of the host of the Men of Rohan, come at last to the rescue of Gondor. The Nazgul, realising that the moment of victory has eluded him for the present, turns and leaves the gate.

[16] from the original brothers, Elros and Elrond, the Half Elven. Elros chose to be human and Elrond became fully immortal as an Elf. Aragorn was descended from the Line of Elros and Arwen was the daughter of Elrond.